Y0-BSZ-951

James's Will-to-Believe Doctrine:
A Heretical View

James's Will-to-Believe Doctrine

A Heretical View

JAMES C. S. WERNHAM

Kingston and Montreal
McGill-Queen's University Press

© McGill-Queen's University Press 1987
ISBN 0-7735-0567-9

Legal deposit 1st quarter 1987
Bibliothèque nationale du Québec

Printed in Canada

Printed on acid-free paper

This book has been published with the help of a grant
from the Canadian Federation for the Humanities,
using funds provided by the Social Sciences and
Humanities Research Council of Canada.

Canadian Cataloguing in Publication Data

Wernham, James C.S.

James's will-to-believe doctrine
Bibliography: p.
Includes index.
ISBN 0-7735-0567-9
1. James, William, 1842–1910. 2. Belief and doubt.
I. Title.
B945.J23W53 1987   121'.6   C87-093275-6

Parts of chapters 5 and 11 have been published in a
different form in "Ayer's James," *Religious Studies*
(Cambridge University Press), September 1976;
"Alexander Bain on Belief," *Philosophy* (Cambridge
University Press), April 1986; and "Bain's Recantation,"
Journal of the History of Philosophy, January 1986.

To Rosemary

Pascal's argument, then, comes to this: If there be a chance that hell exists, I should act as though it existed; for I must not run a needless risk of eternal suffering, any more than incur a certainty of eternal suffering. That may be granted. But when he proceeds to say that to act as if a thing existed is the same as to believe that it exists, and that therefore I must believe in hell absolutely, the fallacy is obvious.

Leslie Stephen

Contents

Introduction

Introduction

Without an orthodoxy there can be no heresies, and it is arguable that there is no received view of James's will-to-believe doctrine. In the secondary literature, one finds a rich diversity of interpretations, even if one limits the survey to fairly recent discussions of it and ignores differences that are differences in detail only. There *is*, nevertheless, an orthodox view of the doctrine and it was blessed by James himself. That view is that the doctrine is a right-to-believe one, that it is about a right, therefore, and that it is about belief. It has much to commend it. Not only does it have James's endorsement, but it makes best sense of the well-advertised opposition of James to Huxley and Clifford. Theirs was an *ethics* of belief, a duty-not-to-believe doctrine. To be opposed, James's had to be an ethics of belief too, had to be either a duty-to-believe or a moral right-to-believe doctrine. Orthodoxy holds that it started as the former and quickly became the latter. A recent postscript to orthodoxy holds that it is not one but two right-to-believe doctrines, one a more and the other a less liberal one. The more liberal of the two is a right-either-to-believe-or-not-to-believe doctrine. The less liberal one is a right-only-to-believe doctrine.[1] The thesis of the following pages is that orthodoxy, with or without that addendum, is mistaken in all of its essential ingredients. It will be argued that James's doctrine is essentially one of "obligation," not just one of "right," and that the obligation is prudential, not moral. If it is about belief at all, it is, then, what Price has called an "*economics* of belief,"[2] not an "ethics of belief." The second part of the thesis is that the doctrine, though nominally about belief, is in fact about one or other of the several things which James, demonstrably, failed to distinguish from belief.

By "James's will-to-believe doctrine," I mean the doctrine expressed in his essay "The Will to Believe" and elsewhere. It is a doctrine which appears at least as early as 1875, and reappears at intervals throughout the roughly twenty-year period following. My first three chapters deal with "beginnings," chapter 1 with James's incautious duty-of-belief remark[3] in his 1875 book review in the *Nation* of Tait's *The Unseen Universe*. Chapters 2 and 3 examine different aspects of his article on the subjective method, written two years later and echoed in some later papers. The thesis is that James's doctrine is, first, a foolish-not-to-believe doctrine and then, when the moral challenge has arisen, a foolish-not-to-believe-and-not-immoral-to-believe one. The argument given by James in support of the doctrine at this stage turns essentially on his claim that some beliefs are self-verifying, a claim illustrated by his story of the Alpine Climber.

My next five chapters consider the famous, or infamous, will-to-believe essay, the first two of them concentrating on his thesis statement in section IV. The main claim of chapter 4 is that a "forced" option is one that we cannot afford not to decide, not one which we cannot avoid deciding. The main claims of chapter 5 are, first, that a "momentous" option is one which we cannot afford to decide in one of the two ways in which we can decide it; and, second, that "cannot ... be decided on intellectual grounds" must mean "cannot *yet* [not cannot *ever*] be decided on intellectual grounds." Chapter 6 examines James's section X where he applies the general thesis of his section IV to the case of religion. The claim is that the doctrine is still a foolish-not-to-believe one, supported now, however, by a new argument. This argument turns on the claim that to have any chance of getting evidence about theism one must first believe it. The paradoxical nature of that claim leads to the topic of chapters 7 and 8, the question whether the essay is really about belief. Some other candidates are uncovered. Among them are being ready to act on theism, gambling on it, and taking it as a working hypothesis.

My last five chapters examine writers other than James on topics basic to my treatment of James. Chapter 9 discusses Clifford's ethics of belief, his duty-not-to-believe doctrine. Chapter 10 deals with Pascal's foolish-not-to-believe claim in the famous pensée "Infini-rien," and raises the question whether the claim is about believing that God exists or about gambling on it. Chapter 11 examines Bain's account of belief and action, a topic crucial to the question whether James's essay is about belief or action. Chapter 12 discusses origins. It agrees with two of James's own verdicts, one that his essay was "cribbed from" Renouvier, the other that it is best not mixed up with pragmatism. Chapter 13 deals with two critics who share the merit of suggesting, in different ways, that James's essay will read better if it can be read as about something other than belief. My conclusion recommends how to read James's doctrine and explains briefly its bearing on our understanding of faith.

My quarrel, I have said, is with orthodoxy; but it is not with orthodoxy only. The recent literature on James boasts, in addition to the received view of him, a multitude of deviant ones. Some of them have so little following as to be no more than curious eccentricities. Others have a currency which is wide enough to make them more than that. It is good policy not to do battle on all fronts at the same time, but that does not rule out a series of quick pre-emptive strikes against other targets before the main battle is joined. That is what will follow in the rest of this introduction. First, however, it is worth recalling how James himself responded to the critics of his time.

He wrote once that he had been "in much hot water lately"[4] over his will-to-believe doctrine. The heat came from different quarters. Some complained that his defence of faith was a defence of something so thin and tepid as not to deserve to be called faith. "Damned if I call it faith!"[5] "Damme if I call that faith, either,"[6] James replied, adding that his own faith was robuster than any variety of it that could be successfully adapted to the conditions of academe. His usual response, however, was to cry "Foul," to claim misrepresentation. For that, he sometimes blamed his title. Had he not labelled his article "The Will to Believe," one critic "would have been without a pretext for most of what he says."[7] As it was, the criticism was wholly off target. "It is a complete *ignoratio elenchi*, and leaves untouched *all* my contentions."[8] When the title was not made the culprit, his response stayed otherwise the same. Another critic was chided for substituting "*a travesty* for which I defy any candid reader to find a single justification in my text."[9] But, if that account of him was bad enough, it was, apparently, not yet as bad as could be, for still another one was "vastly worse," a "really farcical interpretation of my *Will to Believe*."[10] It was a situation that prompted prayer: "and I cry to Heaven to tell me of what insane root my 'leading contemporaries' have eaten, that they are so smitten with blindness as to the meaning of printed texts."[11]

In the main, that response was right; there was misreading and misrepresentation. Still, his rhetoric was a bit excessive. The fault, moreover, was not all on the other side. His statements of his position are often less clear than they needed to be, and his position itself is less clear than he thought it was. Today, he is still in much hot water over his will-to-believe doctrine. The sad thing is that his characteristic response is now no less in order than it was then. There is still occasion to cry "Foul," and to wonder what is "the virus, the insane root, the screw loose (or what), that condemns these fellows to judicial blindness in their reading."[12] That readies things for our promised sallies against the deviants.

James called his lecture "an essay in justification *of* faith, a defence of our right to adopt a believing attitude in religious matters."[13] He was right; what it argued for was faith, religious belief; what it argued against was the veto on faith urged by public relations men for science like Huxley and Clifford. Some commentators have taken a surprisingly different view. One calls the religious upshot of the doctrine "from a logical point of view ... only a theological red herring,"[14] and claims that the deeper message of the essay is "the pragmatic use of language." Both claims are wrong, and badly wrong. The first is like saying of the conclusion of the world's best-known syllogism about Socrates' mortality that it is, from a logical point of view, only an anthropological red herring. The second claim depends on two steps, both of them needed to link "The Will to Believe" to the pragmatic use of language, and both of them false. One is the assumption that James's argument turns on the notion of self-verifying beliefs. The other is the identification of self-verifying beliefs with self-verifying *utterances*. Later, it will be shown that the first assumption is wrong. No argument is needed to show that the other one is. Another commentator endorses part, at least, of the preceding position. The essay, he agrees, is "not primarily a defense of religious belief," but is, rather, a defence of "the active experimentalism of modern science."[15] Not James only, but Huxley and Clifford too, would rightly have read with utter disbelief both that claim and the further one that "James was making a general statement in support of the method of empirical science," not a "fuzzy *ad hoc* concession to self-indulgent piety."[16] There is, of course, something to be said even for errors. James's topic was faith, religious belief. The trouble is that he was never clear what faith is, never clear what he was defending. At times, but not consistently, he identified faith with "working hypothesis."[17] That is what gives a toe-hold grip on reality to descriptions of the essay as a showcase for science.

"Preachers would lay it down as a duty, the duty to embrace the faith; James put it forth not at all as a duty but as a liberty. We are *free* to choose belief. It was not 'You should' but 'You may'."[18] That is how Dickinson Miller represented James's doctrine, and he was following James's lead closely. James came to regret his will-to-believe title. "Would God I had never thought of that unhappy title for my essay."[19] His favourite replacement for it was "The Right to Believe."[20] It had to be "right," not "duty," because there was, he had insisted, an equal right *not* to believe. "Indeed we *may* wait, if we will – I hope you do not think that I am denying that."[21] So it is surprising that some accounts portray him as asserting a duty to believe and a duty to will to believe. It is the more surprising since the authors concede that James, having once written about our being in duty bound to believe, retracted the claim almost immediately and never again repeated it. It is that retraction, they say, that was the mistake. "He should have stuck to his guns!"[22] But those guns were never in his armoury. It is true that his was an "obligation" doctrine, not just a "right" one. That is what tempts one to talk of "duty." But the obligation in James is prudential, not moral. That is what makes all such talk mistaken.

If James regretted the word "will," he had no regrets about "believe." He did say, however, both that religious belief or faith is working hypothesis and that it is gamble, "backing the religious hypothesis against the field."[23] That makes it a good question whether his essay is really about believing p, or about taking it as an hypothesis, or about gambling on it – for these, despite him, are not one and the same. If it is not about believing, it is these others which become prime candidates. It is odd, then, that a recent commentator should say that "James does not appear even to be arguing for belief."[24] That is, surely, an extravagant claim. He gives every appearance of doing just that. It comes as a surprise, also, when he tells us that "the attitude he is trying to justify is ... hope."[25] Perhaps: it is just possible. But, for reasons given and others too, there are other candidates that look more promising.

To complaints that he was "advocating *license* in belief,"[26] James replied that he had "hedged the license to indulge in private over-beliefs with so many restrictions and signboards of danger that the outlet was narrow enough."[27] He was exactly right. The option had to be "genuine," that is, all of "living," "forced" and "momentous," and it had to be undecidable on intellectual grounds. So it is astounding to find commentators still describing his essay as "an unrestricted license for wishful thinking."[28] Unrestricted, the licence certainly was not. While some critics thus ignore restrictions which James carefully wrote in, others also write in restrictions which he deliberately left out. So, while some are sure that he did not restrict his right to believe to genuine and intellectually undecidable options, others are equally sure that he did restrict it to self-verifying beliefs.[29] James called it "travesty." It was, and still is. If there is any excuse for it, it is that he was not always careful to repeat the qualifications built into his formal statement of his thesis, so that there are versions of it that have a liberality far exceeding that of the original. But when a writer insists on eschewing pedantry, it is ungenerous of his readers to capitalize on the omission.

James's famous essay appeared some ninety years ago. It has been widely read,[30] variously read, and, as he claimed, badly read. It would be nice to get it right – especially if it has something worthwhile to tell us about religion.

One last word. Given my thesis, I could not easily avoid criticism of authorities. I have tried in the text to avoid names where I could conveniently do so. Those readers who wish to be assured that there are persons behind the positions criticized in the text will find some help in the notes.

Beginnings

CHAPTER ONE

The Nation *Affair*

"When Dr. William James gets back from his journeys I shall have two bones to pick with him."[1] So wrote Chauncey Wright in his letter to Grace Norton of 12 July 1875. He let no grass grow under his feet. His second letter of six days later reports the deed already done. "I have carried out my purpose of giving Dr. James the two lectures I had in store for him."[2] Wright then gives Mrs Norton, not a blow by blow account, but a reasonably full report of the encounter. It would be ungenerous to say that he crows. The letter does, however, present him as the clear victor and exudes satisfaction in a job well and truly done. The account, clearly, was written while the events were very fresh in his mind, so if there are doubts about its accuracy, there can hardly be a question of failure of memory. Nor is there any question of deliberate misrepresentation. What is open to question is whether Wright really listened to James's case or rightly understood it. There is reason to think that he did not, reason to think, that is, that our primary document contains significant distortion. What is even clearer is that commentators who have explicated Wright's letter have introduced a good deal more. There are, I suggest, two layers of distortion obscuring our view of the events, an original one for which Wright is responsible, and a later one superadded by his commentators. Both need to be removed, but, first, let us be clear about some things which the letter leaves not at all in doubt.

The debate was over more than one affair. As Wright makes clear, there were two bones he had to pick with James, two lectures he had in store for him. He is specific not only about the number but also about the issues. One was James's "doctrine in the *Nation* about the duty of belief."[3] The other was "a book-notice by him, in the *North American Review*, of Wundt's physio-psychology."[4] Wright then identifies the issue arising from the latter. "In a paragraph in which he distinguishes and compliments me among the 'empiricists,' he has so badly misapprehended what the experience philosophy in general holds and teaches, that the compliment to me goes for nothing in mitigation of my resentment."[5] In the one lecture, clearly, he was going to set James straight about the duty of belief, in the other one he was going to set him straight about empiricism. Wright also makes it clear that the two topics were addressed, the two lectures given, on separate occasions. It was the one provoked by James's piece on Wundt which came first, on the Wednesday. The other, the lecture on the duty of belief, did not come until the second meeting, on the Friday. "On Friday evening I saw him again and *introduced* the subject of the 'duty of belief' as advocated by him in the *Nation*."[6]

It has been held that James's duty-to-believe remark was aimed at Wright in particular, that it was his early counterposition to Wright's agnosticism.[7] The claim is without the least foundation, but it is easy to see how it arises. The mechanism is the same one as gives rise to another, equally obvious but less important, mistake. It is this. The debate is sometimes presented as if only one issue were involved. That is done when the commentator is interested in one part of it only, in the controversy, for example, over the duty of belief. When this happens, things which relate to the omitted topic get applied wrongly to the other one. That happens, for example, with the opening by-play about typographical errors.

I have carried out my purpose of giving Dr. James the two lectures I had in store for him. I found him just returned home on Wednesday evening. His father remarked in the course of talk, that he had not found any typographical errors in William's article (an author's *bête noire*). I said that I had read it with interest and had not noticed any *typographical* errors. The emphasis attracted the youth's attention, and made him demand an explanation, which was my premeditated discourse. He referred to the compliment to me. "Made at the expense of my friends," I rejoined. He fought vigorously, not to say manfully; but confessed to having written under irritation.[8]

The events there described took place on the Wednesday. So it was the text of the Wundt notice that was the subject of discussion, not at all the text of the Tait review. Commentators find the story too good to leave out. Detached from its proper context, which is omitted, it gets applied where it does not belong. "In his customary spot on the sofa in the living room of the Quincy Street home, Wright replied to a question from Henry James, Sr, by saying that he 'had found no *typographical* errors' in William's *review of Tait*, and William, as Wright intended, asked for an explanation of this emphasis."[9]

Precisely the same mechanism produces the unfounded claim that James's duty of belief remark was directed against Wright. There is no question at all – the letters make it abundantly clear – that Wright does take personally, does take as an attack on himself, something that James had been saying. He is quite aware he has been a target and he says so. "He has been for some time – in consequence of my preaching, he professes – in a rebellious mood towards the views I argue for; and he has written many private essays or notes on the subject; and very unwisely committed himself to expressions of his animosity in published writings."[10] Nor will his resentment be mollified by James's portraying him as better than most of his kind. "He referred to the compliment to me. 'Made at the expense of my friends,' I rejoined."[11] As we have seen, Wright's report on the Wednesday session ends there, with the summation, "He fought vigorously, not to say manfully; but confessed to having written under irritation."[12]

It was empiricism, then, that was the subject of the Wednesday discussion. In particular, it was James's account of what the experience philosophy holds and teaches, and his charge that, failing to define what experience is, its proponents fail to recognize that experience is conditioned by interests on the part of the subject. The topic that evening was not the duty of belief. That was discussed only on Friday. On Friday, as on Wednesday, Wright is attacking James, but he is not then mounting a counterattack or engaging in self-defence. None of the remarks in which he portrays himself as a target under attack from James occurs in the report on the duty of belief debate. All of them occur when he is reporting the earlier debate on the other subject.

How, then, does one make the case that Wright saw himself as, and was, the particular target in James's remark on the duty of belief? The recipe is now familiar. One notes, correctly, that Wright portrays himself as the target of an attack from James. One mentions no dispute between them but the duty of belief matter. That done, the case looks plausible that the duty of belief remark was the attack on Wright. By restricting the debate to one topic,[13] by omitting part of the original document and joining up things which are separated in it, one obtains a result which seriously distorts the situation as described by Wright. It is, to repeat, on the Wednesday, on the empiricism issue, that Wright takes matters personally, sees himself as under attack. On Friday, when the topic is the duty of belief, there is not the slightest hint of that.

It has been widely held that James affirmed a duty-to-believe doctrine in 1875.[14] Wright certainly thought that he did. One of the lectures he was keeping in store for James on his return concerned his "doctrine in the *Nation* about the duty of belief." He was, moreover, not without excuse for thinking as he did. "Duty bound" is the expression James had used, and that is the language of moral obligation, if anything is. More fully, the offending remark was this:

We for our part not only hold that such an act of trust is licit, but we think, furthermore, that any one *to whom it makes a practical difference* (whether of motive to action or of mental peace) is in duty bound to make it. If 'scientific' scruples withhold him from making it, this proves his intellect to have been simply sicklied o'er and paralysed by scientific pursuits.[15]

A few days later, however, the mistake has been exposed and corrected, and Wright is now much less clearly excusable. His own account of a crucial moment in the debate goes like this. "He retracted the word 'duty'. All that he meant to say was that it is foolish not to believe, or try to believe, if one is the happier for believing."[16] In direct speech, that is: "I retract the word, 'duty'. All I meant to say is that it is foolish not to believe." These are not the words of a man retreating from a position he has held. They are the words of a man retreating from a word, because it misstates his real position. In withdrawing the word "duty," James was acknowledging that it was the wrong word, that it badly expressed what his position really was. It was not his position he was modifying. What he was modifying and correcting was a misleading statement of it. His position when he wrote the *Nation* review was that it is foolish not to believe if one is happier for believing. It had never been anything different. It was still the same now.

Wright, it is abundantly clear, does not act as if that were the case. What he attacks is the *moral* doctrine, the duty of belief doctrine properly so-called. He acknowledges James's retraction of the word "duty": he continues to act as if James really had held the doctrine it expresses. He cannot do otherwise without wrecking his plans. He had come to pick a bone with James over the duty of belief doctrine properly so-called, to lecture him on the errors of that way. It quite ruins his plan and his lecture if James does not hold it. Wright delivers his lecture as planned, and not without some excuse, for, if someone is careless enough to have said "duty" when he did not mean "duty" and has thereby misled one into preparing a lecture against him, he is still somewhat deserving of what was coming to him, even if he has now corrected his former mistake.

It is significant that Wright's report does betray some feeling of unease, a concern that perhaps he is missing something, that perhaps he has not got James's position right. He finds it puzzling that James had affirmed the moral doctrine of a duty to believe if one is the happier for believing. "But even so he seemed to me to be more epicurean (though he hates the sect) than even the utilitarians would allow to be wise."[17] The pity is that he did not allow his quite proper surprise to grow into doubt and then into denial, into a recognition that James's position was really a prudential one, not a moral one.

It has been held that, under pressure from Chauncey Wright, James abandoned his earlier duty-to-believe doctrine for a right-to-believe one. "William James was influenced in many ways by Wright, but from the first he rebelled against his friend's agnosticism. James early proposed a counterposition which he first called the 'duty to believe', but modified simply to the 'right to believe' under Wright's criticism."[18] Clearly, that must be wrong if, as has been argued, James never had a duty-to-believe doctrine, and if, in the debate, what he did was try to make that fact clear. For the sake of argument, however, let us waive these points, already argued. Let us suppose that James was being less than candid in his disclaimer, that he had meant to say exactly what he did say, and that he was, therefore, abandoning a position he had held, while not admitting that he was. For what, then, was he abandoning it? The answer is inescapable that he was abandoning it for a foolish-not-to-believe doctrine. That is the language Wright's letter uses. There is no occurrence of the phrase "right to believe," no occurrence of it in connection with James, no occurrence of it in connection with Wright. So, even if James retreated, the claim is perverse that he retreated to a right-to-believe position. If he modified his position, it was not from a moral duty to a moral right doctrine. It was from a moral "ought" or "obligation" to a prudential "ought" or "obligation" doctrine. The move – if there is any – is not from a stronger to a weaker *moral* claim. It is from a moral to a *prudential* claim. The claim is still about what *ought* to be done. What, if anything, has happened is that the moral "ought" has been replaced by the prudential one.

It has been held that the discussion issued in a meeting of minds, in a common endorsement of a right-either-to-believe-or-not-to-believe doctrine. It has been put this way:

> [W]hen the evidence is genuinely unpersuasive, a person has the *right* to believe anything his natural bent prefers until further evidence is forthcoming. If this natural bent is toward a belief in God, Wright continued, then he has the right to such a belief, just as another person who is not affectively involved in the question of God's existence has an equal right to suspend judgment.[19]

That account, to say the least, is a highly imaginative one. That is not just because there is no occurrence of the phrase "right to believe," in the original text. There is, also, no mention there of "belief in God." The impression that is conveyed in Wright's letter is one of two people talking at cross purposes, talking past one another. James did not budge one inch from his position. Not only is it not foolish to believe, it is foolish not to. That was his thesis. He was talking prudence and nothing more: he was talking obligation and nothing less. Wright appears totally oblivious to that. Not without excuse, he had assumed James was talking ethics. He, therefore, talked ethics too. It is true that he does mention agreements. They were agreed, he says, in rejecting a duty of belief. "He retracted the word 'duty' ... So far we are agreed, and he retracts."[20] They were agreed, he says, that evidence is all that enforces the obligation of belief. That excluded the view that we are obligated to believe by the good consequences of believing, "if one is the happier for believing." They were agreed, also, that attention to all accessible evidence was the only duty involved in belief. That was because belief, as distinct from attention to the evidence, was not a matter of choice, not subject to voluntary control. In sum, Wright got his duty-of-belief lecture off his chest, and James put up no resistance. There was no reason why he should. The attack was all off target. Of course, the moral issue could become relevant. Someone might hold that it was morally wrong to believe on insufficient evidence, even if it was prudent, even if one was happier for so doing. Then the moral challenge would have to be faced. That time was not yet, however. Wright was the bearer of no such challenge. He was no advocate of a duty-not-to-believe doctrine. He was an opponent of it. "And further, I allowed that unproved beliefs, unfounded in evidence, were not only allowable, but were sometimes even *fit, becoming* or *appropriate to* states of feeling or types of character, which are deserving of approval, or even of honor."[21] So, when the moral challenge would come, there was, after all, some comfort James could derive from the sometimes uncomfortable attentions Wright insisted on paying him.

It has been held that James's right-to-believe doctrine, his alleged retreat position of 1875, was the germ of the doctrine which in 1896 "emerged full blown in James's essay, 'The Will to Believe.'"[22] Of course, that has to be false if neither in 1875 nor in 1896 was James's doctrine a right-to-believe one. If the question is put differently, however, if it is whether the foolish-not-to-believe doctrine of 1875 is the germ of his foolish-not-to-believe doctrine of 1896, the answer is undoubtedly that it is. That case cannot be argued quite yet. Worth noticing, however, is an intriguing parallelism in the language of the two texts. "Not only ... licit ... but ... in duty bound" is the language of 1875. "Not only lawfully may but must" is the language of 1896.

To sum up: in 1875 James's ought-to-believe doctrine got off on the wrong foot. James expressed himself badly. Had that not happened, had he not said "duty bound," or had Wright let him revoke the phrase, as he tried to do, the waters would have been less muddied than they have become. Led by Wright, critics have seen James advancing a moral thesis he never did hold, a moral ought-to-believe doctrine. They have seen him retreating from that position when in reality his position did not change at all. Just how consistent James was in affirming his prudential ought-to-believe doctrine we shall see as the story unfolds.

CHAPTER TWO

Message from the Mountains

Late in 1877 James sent off to France an expanded exposition of his ought-to-believe doctrine. He had reason to anticipate a good reception for it, and he was not disappointed. The editor of *Critique Philosophique*[1] was enthusiastic about the new work. It was, he said, a very remarkable paper, consonant – as James himself had more than hinted – with views espoused by the journal, but fresh and original in its presentation. He did, indeed, concede that readers might have reservations here or there, or need for clarification, but, as far as he was concerned, the paper was a winner. Written by James in French, it was published in 1878, after some polishing by Renouvier, as "Quelques Considérations sur la Méthode Subjective." Had Wright been still alive, he would certainly have echoed the comment about reservations and the need for clarification. He would not, one suspects, have echoed the note of enthusiasm. Wright had died suddenly in 1875. In the *Nation*, James paid him an elegant, moving, and affectionate tribute, recognizing in him "a character of which his friends feel more than ever now the elevation and the rarity."[2] It was not all eulogy, however. "Never in a human head was contemplation more separated from desire."[3] That comment was meant critically, although Wright would not have taken it so. It is James's case against that separation of head and heart that is the burden of his paper on the subjective method.

Wright's death was not the only notable event to have occurred in the interval. The moral challenge had been sounded with a veritable blast of trumpets. In January of 1877, Clifford's "The Ethics of Belief" had been published in *Contemporary Review*. Its central thesis is the moral claim that "it is wrong always, everywhere, and for anyone, to believe anything upon insufficient evidence."[4] In the spring of the same year, Huxley had raised the level of stridency, condemning, not just as wrong but as the lowest depths of immorality, believing, because of the utility of so doing, what one has no ground at all for believing. It is possible that James did know of Clifford's paper and that his own one was occasioned by it. It is hardly likely, however, since he gives no sign of any acquaintance with it. He was, however, certainly aware of Huxley's pronouncement and paraphrased it neatly, improving somewhat on the original. "Croire parce qu'on voudrait croire serait faire preuve de la dernière immoralité."[5] Believing just because of a desire to believe – that was letting desire trespass upon the preserve of contemplation: it was mixing the heart into what was the proper business of the head. What makes James's paraphrase superior is that it makes clearer than the original had done, that it was believing, not just pretending to believe, that had aroused Huxley's moral indignation. The original was this: "so long as they hold by the plain rule of not pretending to believe what they have no reason to believe because it may be to their advantage so to pretend, they will not have reached the lowest depths of immorality."[6]

James's paper on the subjective method is a paper on wishful-thinking. He advocates it, not in all circumstances of course, but in some.[7] So he could have called the paper "In Support of Wishful Thinking." That would have sounded less philosophical, but it would not have been less fitting. The place to begin, however, is not with the subjective method, but with its rival. The objective method is the view that one ought to believe only in accordance with the evidence. One ought to believe p when the evidence favours p. One ought to believe not-p when the evidence favours not-p. When the evidence favours neither side, what one ought to do is withhold belief, suspend judgment, until such time as there is a balance of evidence. Sometimes it is held that the "ought," the obligation, is moral. More commonly, it is held to be not moral but prudential. The case is that if we believe what the evidence favours, we believe what is likely to be true; and, further, that action guided by true belief is more likely to promote our goals than action guided by false belief, or unguided by any belief. A belief not supported by the evidence may be true; an action not guided by a true belief may promote our goal. That is admitted. The claim made is that, nevertheless, the policy of believing only what the evidence favours is the prudent policy, the policy one ought prudentially to follow. James accepts that claim – subject to one rider. The rider is that when a belief is self-verifying, the prudent thing is to believe what one wants to be true.

It would be nice to have a more positive and more precise account of the subjective method than the one just given. The fact is, however, that the term covers a variety of claims which have little in common but their opposition to the objective method. At different stages of his paper, James champions each of the following positions:

1 We have a right not to believe what the evidence favours.

2 We have an obligation to believe what no balance of evidence favours.
3 We have an obligation to believe what the evidence is against.

Each of these contradicts some part of the objective method. The first denies its claim that one ought always to believe what the evidence favours. The second denies its claim that one ought always to withhold belief when there is no balance of evidence. The third, the most radical, not only denies, as the first one does, that one ought always to believe what the evidence favours, but asserts an obligation to believe what the evidence is against. A case for any one of these claims would be a case for the subjective method. A case for the first one only would be a case for a right-not-to-believe doctrine. A case for either of the others would be a case for an ought-to-believe doctrine. What James promises is support for a right-not-to-believe doctrine. What his paper delivers is support for an ought-to-believe one. That somewhat dogmatic description we can now tie a bit more closely to the three stages of his paper.

His question, James tells us at the outset, is the question "si l'on est en droit de repousser une théorie confirmée en apparence par un nombre très-considérable de faits objectifs, uniquement parce qu'elle ne répond point à nos préférences intérieures."[8] The positivists and leading scientists of the day have their answer, he tells us: they say there is no such right. His own position has been, and still is, that there is such a right, and his paper will set out the case for that position. The case to be given, in sum, is for a right, not for an obligation (si l'on est en droit de); it is for a right not to believe (repousser une théorie); and it is for a right not to accept despite the presence of a favourable balance of evidence (confirmée en apparence par un nombre très-considérable de faits objectifs). What James delivers is something different. At the heart of his paper is his story of the Alpine Climber. It will occupy us presently, and for some time. It affirms, we shall see, his second position, his ought-to-believe-despite-the-absence-of-evidence doctrine. The first part of that claim, that the story asserts an obligation to believe not just a right, will be argued in a moment. The other part, the part about the absence of evidence, is clear at once from the text: "j'ignore, faute d'expérience, si j'en aurai la force."[9] "Being without similar experience, I have no evidence of my ability to perform it successfully."[10] The Alpine Climber, the claim will be, ought to believe he can make the leap; he ought to believe it, and not suspend judgment, despite his having no ground for believing it. In the rest of the paper, when James returns to metaphysics from the mountains, his position changes to the third one. There the claim will be that we ought to believe despite the presence of an unfavourable balance of evidence. We ought, as we shall see in the next section, to be optimists and libertarians, in spite of the fact that we do have grounds for disbelieving these views.

Our present concern, however, is with the Alpine Climber. The story goes like this.[11] A.C. (the Alpine Climber) has found himself in a place where he can save his life only by making a difficult leap. There is no ground for believing he can make it, nor ground either for believing that he cannot. According to the objective method, then, what he must do is withhold belief, suspend judgment. He does not. He believes he can make it and he finds that he can. Had he not believed that, he would not have been able to do it. Put in another way which brings out better the self-verifying nature of his belief, the essentials of the story are these. A.C. believes the proposition, p. P is true if the situation, s, occurs. His believing p causes s to occur and, thereby, causes p to be true. Had he not believed p, s would not have occurred, and p would not have been true. A.C.'s belief that he can make it, in short, is a self-verifying one.

There is more than one lesson we are to take from that story. The primary, the principal one is certainly this; that A.C. would have been a fool not to believe he could make it. He perishes if he believes he cannot. He perishes if he suspends judgment. He saves himself only if he believes. In the language of James's Tait review, A.C.'s believing is not only licit, but, in his situation, any one who prizes his life is bound to believe he can make the leap. Bound, but not duty bound. This time James avoids his earlier mistake. To believe what one wants to be true, to wishful-think, is, he says, "the part of wisdom."[12] Not to do so would be "trebly assinine."[13] "Je ne serais qu'un sot si je ne crois pas ce que je désire."[14] If A.C. thinks he will not make it, he will not; if he thinks he will, he will. So, either belief is self-verifying. It is the second one only, however, which is expedient. "Toute la différence entre les deux cas, c'est que le second vous est fort avantageux."[15] James's language is clear and consistent. It is an ought-to-believe doctrine, and the "ought" is prudential, not moral.

There is a second lesson we are to take from the story. It is that in what A.C. did, there was nothing morally wrong at all. That is the other part of James's message; without it, he would have been ignoring Huxley, not answering him. Huxley's objection was that wishful thinking was morally wrong, even when it was expedient. James is almost content to let A.C.'s case speak for itself. There are not many places where his language is unambiguously the language of morality. There is one, however, and it shows that the moral challenge was not being left unanswered. Where beliefs are not self-verifying, he conceded to the opposition, wishful-thinking, the subjective method, *is* imprudent and immoral. "Elle ne serait que pernicieuse, et il faut même dire immorale ..."[16] The message is that when they *are* self-verifying, wishful thinking is not imprudent and not immoral either. That settles the expository question. The prudential ought-to-believe doctrine is joined now by a moral right-to-believe one. There still remains the critical question, the question whether the story can support the thesis James rests on it. To answer it, we need to be clearer about self-verifying beliefs. We also need to know whether the verdict passed on A.C.'s case – that he would be foolish not to believe he can make it – depends only on its having the self-verifying feature, or on its having certain other features as well. In the latter case, the thesis will require to be given a more guarded expression. First, however, about self-verification.

There are three things worth noting about A.C.'s case. The first is that his belief is, as James puts it, a factor in and not just a confessor of the truth that he can.[17] It creates its own verification, makes itself true, he says sometimes. It helps create its own verification, helps make itself true, he says at other times.[18] It is a factor in the outcome and no belief is a self-verifying one unless that is true of it. The second is that his belief is verified. He does make it, so it is true that he can. Suppose, however, that he had not made it. His belief still enables him to make a better attempt than otherwise he could have made. It falls short, however, of what was needed. His belief was a factor. It did not, however, create its own verification or make itself true. It did not, because it was not verified, was not made true. For the same reason, it did not help create its own verification, or help make itself true. It was a factor, and a factor *making for* the truth of p, but not, now, a factor making or helping to make p true. The third thing about A.C.'s case is this; he would not have been able to make the leap if he had not believed he could. Suppose, however, that he would. He believes he can make it. His belief enables him to make a better leap than otherwise he could have made. It is, then, a factor. He does better as a result of believing. His belief, moreover, was verified. He does make it, and so it is true that he can. What, now, is also true is that he can make it without believing, that he can make it any way. We need to know whether A.C.'s belief is self-verifying only in the actual case, or whether it also is in the supposed cases. We need to know, in other words, whether or not a belief is self-verifying, only if it shares all of the three listed features of A.C.'s case.

The fact is that James does not tell us. He sticks closely to his paradigm. "Ne croyez pas, vous aurez raison; et, en effet, vous tomberez dans l'abîme. Croyez, vous aurez encore raison, car vous vous sauverez."[19] That is true in the actual case. It is not true in our two supposed cases. In the first of these he will not save himself even if he believes. In the second, he will not save himself only if he believes. James says enough to suggest the questions we have raised, but not enough to answer them. "Cette foi peut tromper, très bien. Les efforts dont elle me rend capable peuvent ne pas aboutir à créer un ordre de choses qu'elle entrevoit et voudrait déterminer."[20] That is what happens in the first of our cases. The belief is not verified. James does not add that in that case the belief is no longer a self-verifying one. "Je crois ce que je désire; ma confiance me donne des forces et rend possible ce qui, sans elle, ne l'eût peut-être pas été."[21] Then, perhaps it would have been possible any way. That is what happens in our second case. He would have been able to do it anyway, without believing. Again, James does not add that the belief, then, is not a self-verifying one. No belief is self-verifying unless it makes for its own truth. That much is made clear. What is left in some doubt is whether that condition is sufficient as well as necessary. It is plausible to think James held that it was. He had ample opportunity to say that it was not, if he thought so, and it was certainly important to do that. As already remarked, he did no such thing. Moreover, he wants the term, "self-verifying," to apply widely. He calls the class of self-verifying beliefs "immense" and "enormous,"[22] and it applies more widely the fewer the conditions that are built into it. It is plausible, then, to take him to mean that a belief is self-verifying if, like the belief of A.C., it makes for its own verification, even if it does not share the other listed features of that case. In that case, the thesis is not, or not just, that when thinking makes it so it is folly not to believe. The thesis is that it is folly not to believe when thinking makes for its being so.

The question, then, is whether the story will support that thesis. The answer is that it will not. Consider the following. Our verdict that A.C. would be foolish not to believe depends on some special features of the case, features not always co-present with the self-verifying one. A.C., it is clear, would be foolish not to try the leap. That is because of the conjunction of two things. One is that he has no chance if he does not. No helicopter will hover overhead dangling a lifeline. No fully equipped St Bernard will lead a rescue party up the slope. The other is that he has some chance if he tries. The distance is six feet, not sixty. Change one of these and our verdict also changes. Suppose he does have a chance if he does nothing, if he just sits tight; suppose there is some chance the search and rescue team will chalk up another success. Even if he does have a chance if he jumps, we may well think that it would not be at all foolish of him not to try it. Now change the other one as well. He has a chance if he sits tight and none if he jumps. The distance is not six feet but sixty. In that case we should certainly say that he would be foolish to try, not just that he would not be foolish not to.

But what of believing? The answers stay much the same. Suppose, in each case, that believing improves one's level of performance. In the original case, unamended, our verdict remains still the same; it would be foolish not to try, believing. In the case, as first amended, where now he does have a chance if he sits tight, we should say that it is not foolish of him to do just that, not foolish, therefore, not to try, believing. In the final case, we should judge both that it would be foolish to try, *and* that it would be foolish to try, believing. If the leap is one of six feet, our belief may well decide between success and failure. But not if it is sixty. Confidence is, no doubt, a fine thing, but it does not turn us into Superman or Wonderwoman.

In his paper on the subjective method, then, James reaffirmed his foolish-not-to-believe doctrine of 1875, tying it to the class of self-verifying beliefs. He also recognized and rejected the moral challenge trumpeted by Huxley. Renouvier's remark was, however, a perceptive one. There *was* need for clarification. The central notion of self-verification needed to be made clearer than it was. When that is done, there is, also, ample room for reservation about the position James took. That is so even if attention is limited, as so far it has been, to James's illustration, to his story of A.C. The criticism is much more in order when we pass from that story to the message which he took it to have for metaphysics.

CHAPTER THREE

From Mountaineering to Metaphysics

The story of A.C. was not meant for climbers only. Its lesson was for all of us. In part, it was a reply to Huxley's ethics of belief. First and foremost, however, it was a prudential justification of the subjective method, a justification of wishful thinking. The subjective method had no place, James was quick to agree, where belief is a confessor only, not a factor. It was, however, the right method in metaphysics, for metaphysical beliefs, or some of them, were self-verifying ones. That is not, on the face of it, a very promising thesis. A.C.'s belief was a belief about himself, and so are the other examples of self-verifying beliefs that come most readily to mind. So it is tempting to think that the only self-verifying beliefs are self-regarding ones. If that is rejected, on the ground that one person's belief in another person may be self-verifying, it still remains plausible that the only self-verifying beliefs are beliefs about persons. If James wants to hold, then, that all metaphysical beliefs are self-verifying, he must refute that position or hold that they are all, somehow, about persons. If his thesis is the more modest one that some metaphysical beliefs are self-verifying, he will have to hold that these particular ones are about persons. At times, he appears to champion the stronger view. It is, however, only the more modest one which gets worked out in any detail. In his paper on the subjective method, the topics which feature are optimism and pessimism, idealism and materialism, and freedom and determinism. The first of these appears again in "The Sentiment of Rationality" and in "Is Life Worth Living?"[1] The discussions in them are similar to the one in the earlier text. The second topic reappears also in "The Sentiment of Rationality," where the treatment again resembles part of the discussion in the earlier text, but is quite silent on the self-verifying claim. It is hard to think that the silence is entirely accidental. The discussion in the earlier paper suggests that idealism and materialism are less easily portrayed as self-verifying beliefs than are optimism and pessimism.

Optimism and Pessimism

The first question is how James uses the terms. Renouvier's footnote to the text does not help matters.[2] His suggestion is that James is not using "optimism" in the way standard in theodicy and in the philosophy of history. He was not using it, that is, for the view that all is good, all is necessary. Rather, he used "pessimism" for the view that everything is evil, and "optimism" for the contradictory of that view, not for its contrary. It comes to this; that James meant by "optimism" the claim that not everything is bad, not the claim that everything is good. It is an odd suggestion. Few pessimists hold that nothing is good, and one does not qualify as an optimist by holding that the world is not all bad. For that kind of optimism no argument is necessary. It is different if optimism is the view that reality is all good, good through and through. It is different, also, if it is the view that reality is more good than bad, good on the whole. These claims need argument for they are controversial ones. The same is not true of the claim that some things are good. Renouvier's suggestion is not only odd, however; it is also mistaken. For James, optimism is the view that reality is, if not perfect, perfectible; and despite Renouvier, the argument he gives for it is part of the stock-in-trade of works on theodicy. He does, indeed, add his special twist – the self-verifying thesis – but the rest of the case is absolutely standard.

James remarks that in Germany pessimism had become an article of faith;[3] and it is worth going back to a short piece he had written in 1875 on "German Pessimism."[4] The self-verifying thesis is there already; so, also, is a definition of optimism. The definition needs some elucidation, some revision even, but the drift is obvious enough to be unmistakeable. First, we get the self-verifying thesis, "we may not talk of its *being* true, but *becoming* true. Its full verification must be contingent on our complicity both theoretical and practical."[5] Then comes the definition of optimism. "All that it asserts is that the facts of the world are a fit basis for the *summum bonum*, if we do our share and react upon them as it is meant we should (with fortitude, for example, and undismayed hope). The world is thus absolutely good only in a potential or hypothetic sense."[6] The term used there is "absolutely good"; in the paper on the subjective method, it is "the best of worlds."[7] That is enough, perhaps, to settle the case against Renouvier. The two texts are mutually illuminating, however, and staying with them a little longer will show just how standard is James's case, at least in part.

The following points are by way of commentary.

1 The phrase "the facts of the world" has to be understood not as an equivalent for "all facts," but rather as what, in the other text, James symbolizes as M, the mass of facts which is independent of us. "All facts" is represented as M+R, where R stands for those facts which are dependent on us, our reactions and their consequences.

2 When James says that the facts of the world are a fit basis for the summum bonum, if we react to them in certain ways, his expression needs correction. He means that they are a fit basis for the summum bonum no matter how we react to them. It is the realization of the summum bonum which requires that we react in a certain way.

3 When he says that, according to optimism the world is absolutely good in a potential or hypothetical sense, what he means is that the facts of the world, or M, are not such as to exclude the whole's being absolutely good; put another way, that the whole, or M+R, *can be* absolutely good, and that whether it will be or not depends on the nature of R. It is important to be clear what it is that optimism is a belief about. We can say of M that it is capable of being part of the best possible world. That will not serve as a definition of optimism, for the same M, James says, is no less capable of being part of the worst possible: "M en soi est ambigu, capable, selon le complément qu'il recevra, de figurer dans un pessimisme ou dans un optimisme moral."[8] Further, it is *now* true that M is capable of being part of a world that is absolutely good. That is not something that is yet to be made true; so, optimism, defined in that way could not be self-verifying. In sum, optimism has to be a belief about M+R, the view that the world of which M forms a part is the best possible. As such it is a belief whose truth-value is indeterminate, and that, of course, is a sine qua non of its being a self-verifying one.

4 As James puts it, "tout dépend du charactère de R."[9] Another way of saying, then, that M+R can be absolutely good, and will be absolutely good, or not, depending on our response, is to say that *we can make* M+R absolutely good. That way of putting it brings out that optimism is a belief about persons, at least in part.

5 By what is it that we make M+R absolutely good? By the nature of our response, James answers. If, for example, hardship or infirmity evoke from us a response of bitterness, envy, self-pity, they become parts of a greater evil than would have been possible without them. If, on the other hand, we meet our trials with the heroic virtues, then they become parts of a greater good than would have been possible without them. "Nul rayon dans cette nuit"[10] is how James describes his first case. "No shadow in that brightness," he might have said of the other. In effect, he combines the two in his remark that M is indeterminate and, depending on the complement it gets, can be part of the worst or of the best.

So far the case could be matched from virtually any theodicy. Both the claim itself and the supporting argument are absolutely standard. There is, also, of course, his special twist. As he said, the truth of optimism requires not just our practical but our theoretical complicity as well. It requires the theoretical, he means, because it requires the practical. The world, in short, is perfectible, and we can perfect it, but only if we believe we can.

The second question is how James justifies the move from mountaineering to metaphysics, from A.C.'s leap to optimism. The answer is that he simply takes the cases to be analogous. In both of them alike, everything is made to depend on our response and our response is made to depend on our belief. A passage in "Is Life Worth Living?" displays the case as well as any. It begins with the story of A.C. and draws the now familiar, but extravagant lesson. "Refuse to believe, and you shall indeed be right, for you shall irretrievably perish. But believe, and again you shall be right, for you shall save yourself."[11] Then comes the claim that warrants the transition. The question of pessimism, "the question whether life is worth living is subject to conditions logically much like these."[12] "Much like," he says, not "just like"; but it is clear that he would not have balked at the other expression. The passage continues; "If your surrender to the nightmare view and crown the evil edifice by your own suicide, you have indeed made a picture totally black."[13] Believe the worst, and it will be so; believe the best, and that will be so. Just as you can save your life if you believe you can, and only if you believe, so you can perfect the world if, and only if, you believe you can. The two cases are presented to us as identical ones. The conclusion then follows that, in the one case as in the other, we should be fools not to believe.

There is more than one difficulty with that case. It trades on the lack of clarity already noted in the notion of self-verification. We agreed that A.C. would be a fool not to believe he could succeed. That was not because believing would assure his success. It was not because withholding belief would assure his failure. The claim that a belief is self-verifying entails neither of these. What is entailed is that believing will improve whatever chance one has of succeeding. That is all, but it is something. In some circumstances, it is enough to warrant the claim that one would be a fool not to believe. It is not enough to warrant that claim in other cases. In his circumstances, A.C. would be a fool not to try the leap and not to try it, believing. Change the circumstances, however, and the verdict, as we have seen, also changes.

Another difficulty with the transition is that the cases are far from identical. Consider just two points. Making the leap is something which A.C. does singlehandedly. Whether he succeeds or fails depends on him and on no one else. Perfecting my life may be something which I do single-handedly, but perfecting the world certainly is not. It depends on

me, and crucially. It requires from me an unbroken stream of moral
victories over the trials of life. It depends just as crucially on everyone
else. It requires of them, too, a similar unbroken succession of moral
victories. Everything depends only on me in the one case, but not in the
other. More important; believing I can perfect my life is not like A.C.'s
believing he can make the leap. His leap was challenging, no walkover,
not obviously makeable; it was not obviously unmakeable either, not, for
example, metres more than the world's record for the long jump. Had it
been that, we should not have said either that he would be a fool not to try
or that he would be a fool not to believe. To believe I can perfect my life
is, however, to think I can break the world's moral record and do it by a
handy margin. Not only so, it is to believe what has already been falsified.
Whatever my success rate may be from now on, it has not been perfect
to this point. The same, no doubt, is true of everyone else. Optimism, in
short, is a very different case from A.C.'s belief, and one cannot use one
of them as a paradigm for the other. The question of the world's
perfectibility is no longer open. A perfect world is not *now* a *maybe*,[14] if
ever it was, and now, at least, it is foolish to think that it is.

Idealism and Materialism

The second of the metaphysical questions which James discusses need
not detain us so long. It is the question whether the world is at bottom
moral or non-moral, a question which he equates with the question of
materialism. The application of the notion of self-verifying beliefs does
not come immediately. Two questions intervene. One is the question
whether the positivists are right in rejecting the question as a meaningless
one. James argues that they are not right. The other is whether it can be
known *now* whether or not materialism is true, and if not, when and how
it will be known. His answer is that the method of truth testing is the same
as that for any scientific hypothesis; only, the time it will take is very
much greater. Elsewhere, he suggests that we should not expect the issue
to be decided until "the final integration of things, when the last man has
had his say."[15] So far in the discussion, there is no mention of
self-verifying beliefs. That comes only in the last four paragraphs,
introduced by the words, "Je peux aller plus loin."[16] That further step, as
noted earlier, is absent from the otherwise similar discussion in "The
Sentiment of Rationality," and the fact may well indicate that James had
second thoughts about it. When the move does come, it comes in the
form of rhetorical questions. Why should materialism and its opposite
not be self-verifying beliefs? What is to prevent M from being in itself
indeterminate and capable, depending on our response, of being part of a
moral or a non-moral universe? Clearly, these questions add up to a claim

essentially like the one made earlier in connection with optimism. There are some noteworthy differences, however. The position taken is a much weaker one. Before, it was that if we believe and act thus and so, the universe will be good. Now it is that if we believe and act thus and so, it is conceivable that it will be a moral universe: "Le cas est concevable."[17] That is as far as James will go here. Another difference is that this case is presented devoid of supporting argument. The reader is simply challenged to say why it cannot be so. He is, indeed, handed an objection, that the character of a totality so vast cannot depend significantly on something so small as our beliefs and doings. James is ready with his answer. The small word "not" can completely change the sense of a whole sentence, a feather can tip the balance when two great weights are in equilibrium. Discussion at that level is less than helpful, and, of course, counterargument to argument against the case in no way compensates for the absence of argument for it. Yet another difference is that, in this case, the question itself remains quite obscure. If we believe there are things which we morally ought to do, and act accordingly, reality in some part of it is moral, as it is not if we believe otherwise and act in accordance with that other belief. That is a truism, and it is surely not for it that James is contending? He has already claimed that M is a fit basis for the summum bonum, that it is not such as to make the moral life impossible. It is surely not just a repetition of that earlier claim that is now being made. Elsewhere, he presents the question of materialism as the issue between moral subjectivism on the one hand and moral objectivism and absolutism on the other.[18] That account makes the question of materialism a different one from the earlier question of pessimism. It is hard to see, however, that James does anything to support a claim that believing moral principles to be subjective helps make them so, or that believing them to be objective or absolute does something to make that so. He argues that believers in these theories will act differently, believers in objectivity will take moral values seriously, while believers in subjectivity will tend not to. That view is probably wrong, but the point is not crucial. If it were true, it would follow that the universe would be morally the better for our believing that moral principles are objective – even if that were false. It would do nothing, however, to show that the one belief, or the other, was self-verifying.

Freedom and Determinism

Before concluding, James touches on yet another case, the question of freedom. His discussion of it need detain us hardly at all. The claim he makes is this one: if free acts are at all possible, their occurrence and their frequency will depend on our believing that they are possible.[19] As a contribution to the metaphysical question of freedom, that takes us nowhere. It may have a bearing on the practical question how to act freely, given that one can. The metaphysical question, however, is the one shrouded in the antecedent of James's hypothetical claim. It is the question whether free acts are possible, together, of course, with the complex of conceptual issues which need to be clarified before that question itself becomes clear.

To conclude: early in his career, James thought he could get much mileage from the notion of self-verifying beliefs. He could exploit it in two ways. He could use it to justify the subjective method in metaphysics, to justify believing what you want to be true. There were limits to that, of course, but they were generous enough to permit the claim that one ought to believe – that it would be foolish not to believe – in the perfectibility of things, in metaphysical roots for morality and in freedom. He could use it, that is, to support his foolish-not-to-believe doctrine of 1875. He could use it, also, to combat the excessive moral severity which proclaimed it always wrong to believe on insufficient evidence. When beliefs are self-verifying, it is both foolish not to believe what you want to be true, and not immoral to believe it. In "The Will to Believe," the thesis, we shall see, is still the same, still a foolish-not-to-believe-and-not-immoral-to-believe one. Also, appeal is still made there to the notion of self-verifying beliefs. In that essay, however, the case for belief in God is supported by a quite different argument. That argument will concern us soon. Now it is enough to say that no claim is made that thinking that God exists will make it so, or even help.[20]

The Will to Believe

CHAPTER FOUR

Forced Options

"The Will to Believe" got less than rave notices. A friend called it "one tissue of ingenious sophistry from outset to end."[1] Some critics have been even less enthusiastic. Ready to endorse "sophistry," they have not been ready to endorse "ingenious." In our time, one has called it "a congeries of egregious errors,"[2] another "an unwitting compendium of common fallacies and a manual of self-deception."[3] For the bad reception, James blamed his choice of title; he should not have used "Will." The best choice, he concluded, would have been "The Right to Believe."[4] That shows he thought his essay was about a right, not about an obligation. What follows is an attempt to show that James's second thoughts about his title were not much better than his first ones, that the doctrine of this paper, also, is a foolish-not-to-believe one. The evidence will be drawn almost exclusively from sections IV and X. To allay fears that an attention so narrowly selective is bound to be a distorting one, let us see where James himself puts the emphasis. That is not difficult, for his essay comes complete with an unusually full set of directions for the reader.

In his opening paragraph, James says what his essay is to be about. It is to be "an essay in justification of faith," or, more fully, "a defence of our right to adopt a believing attitude in religious matters."[5] In section I, he introduces a series of definitions, and warns us not to lose sight of them. In sections II and III, he discusses the psychology of human opinion, concluding that by no means all of our beliefs are founded on evidence. In the short but important section IV, he raises the question whether that fact – that many of our beliefs are not based on evidence – is simply reprehensible and pathological, and he presents his thesis that it is not. That thesis statement he describes as "abstract," and he indicates that it will be made clearer later. Section V is introduced as "a bit more of preliminary work,"[6] and that same description is clearly meant to extend to section VI. Section VII is said to deal with "one more point, small but important" before "our preliminaries are done."[7] Consistently, section VIII describes all the preceding as "all this introduction," and then promises to "go straight at our question."[8] That promise is hardly kept, or kept only minimally. Section VIII repeats the claims made in sections II, III and IV, but immediately turns aside to allay imagined suspicions. It does so by agreeing that the attitude of sceptical balance is the only wise one when there is no forced option. The section ends asking if there are forced options among our speculative questions, and section IX opens with the answer that there are. It then claims, with illustrations, that some beliefs are self-verifying, and asserts that "where faith in a fact can help create the fact," it is "an insane logic" which counsels waiting for the evidence.[9] Section X begins by drawing the conclusion that "faith based on desire is certainly a lawful and possibly an indispensible thing" in relation to "truths dependent on our personal action."[10] It does not proceed to assume that religious claims are so dependent. It objects, rather, that they are not, suggesting that a wide gulf separates "all childish human cases" from the "great cosmical matters like the question of religious faith."[11] Nowhere, in what follows, is anything said to rebut that objection. Finally, section X provides the long delayed claim that the thesis of section IV applies to the religious option, and draws the conclusion that the religious question is one which our passional nature lawfully may and must decide. The argument, in short, turns on sections IV and X. Section IV makes the general claim with no mention made of religion. Section X brings the religious option under the general claim, and together they make the case for religious belief.

Although not everything, James's thesis statement is a major part of the whole and it is the place to begin. It consists of a single sentence, introduced by the words, "The thesis I defend is, briefly stated, this: ... " It is divided in the middle by a semi-colon. Its first half asserts:

Our passional nature not only lawfully may, but must, decide an option between propositions, whenever it is a genuine option that cannot by its nature be decided on intellectual grounds.

The second half adds the following explanation:

for to say, under such circumstances, "Do not decide, but leave the question open," is itself a passional decision, – just like deciding yes or no, – and is attended with the same risk of losing the truth.[12]

That sentence, although not very brief, is briefer than it needed to be. It bought brevity at the cost of clarity. For that, James promised a remedy, saying that all would soon become quite clear. In that, he was oversanguine. Enough obscurity remained to generate widely different accounts of his meaning. Our question – whether James's paper asserts a right or an obligation – turns on the phrase, "not only lawfully may, but must." Other parts of the statement have a bearing on that one, however, so the thing to do is to work our way through it selectively, picking out whatever has light to shed.

First, however, a proposal about terminology. When we decide something on intellectual grounds, it is *we* who decide it, not some part of us called our intellectual nature. When we decide something otherwise than on intellectual grounds, it is again we who decide it, not some other part of us called our passional nature. It will help, then, to alter James's idiom accordingly. Instead of talking of one's intellectual nature or one's passional nature deciding something, let us talk of *our* deciding it, either on intellectual grounds or not on intellectual grounds. Let us note, also, that if we decide something, we decide it either on intellectual grounds or not on intellectual grounds. There is no third way of deciding an option. There is, of course, another way of dealing with it. We can suspend judgment, not decide it. That, however, is obviously not another way of deciding it.

James's claim – that when an option is genuine and undecidable on intellectual grounds, our passional nature not only may but must decide it – includes the following components:

1 that we lawfully may decide it,
2 that we must decide it, and
3 that we lawfully may and must decide it otherwise than on intellectual grounds.

It is clear enough that (3) depends upon (2) and (1). We must decide it otherwise than on intellectual grounds, if it is undecidable on intellectual ones, and if we must decide it. Similarly, we lawfully may decide it otherwise than on intellectual grounds, if it is undecidable on intellectual ones, and if we lawfully may decide it. What is less clear, and more important, is whether (1) depends upon (2). It may, and will do, if what is meant is that we lawfully may decide it if it is true that we must decide it, if it just is not possible for us to do anything else. The principle is that what cannot be avoided cannot be forbidden, that what is unavoidable is allowable. Read in that way, the thesis statement asserts a right to decide, but no more than a right. It says nothing about an obligation. What it does is base the right to decide upon the necessity of deciding, upon the impossiblity of doing anything else.

That is not the only way, perhaps not the natural way, to read the sentence. The other is to take the "lawfully" as carrying over from the "may" to the "must," to read it as asserting that we not only lawfully may but lawfully must decide. To say that we "lawfully may" do something is to say that it is allowed, that no law prohibits it. To say that we "lawfully must" do it is to assert the stronger claim that some law requires it. On the second reading, the "may" claim is quite independent of the "must" one, and the statement asserts more than just a right to decide. It asserts an obligation to do so. We have, in short, two different ways of taking the thesis statement. One makes it assert a right-to-decide doctrine, the other an ought-to-decide one. So the next question is whether there is any reason to prefer either reading to the other.

There is a prima facie case for the first one. It is what James says about "forced" options. If a forced option is one which it just is not possible for us not to decide, then it is one which we must decide in the sense of "must" which the first reading requires – the "must" of necessity – and which the second one excludes. James's account of forced options describes them in precisely that way. That is the first thing to be said. The second is that the way James actually employs the term is very different indeed from the way he says he employs it.

In section 1, he says that an option is forced when it is not avoidable, gives examples of forced and avoidable options, and ends with the statement, "Every dilemma based on a complete logical disjunction, with no possibility of not choosing, is an option of this forced kind."[13] To be a forced one, then, an option must meet two conditions. The first is that the alternatives must comprise a complete logical disjunction. Provided they do, I must choose one or the other, *if I choose*. The second is that there must be no possibility of not choosing. So, an option is a forced one only if it is unavoidable that I choose one or the other if I choose, and if it is unavoidable that I choose. Now consider the term "option." Suppose that we take the option to be this; to believe p or not-p? The first of our two conditions is met. If I believe, I must believe one or the other of those two. It is less clear that such an option meets the second condition. Surely I can always avoid an option of that kind, for I can suspend judgment, believing neither of them. There is always that possibility, or so it would seem, of not believing. Suppose, then, that we take the option differently, to be whether or not to believe p. That option cannot be avoided by suspending judgment. That is because suspending judgment is a way of not believing p. So, on James's definition, any option that is forced has to be of the kind, to believe p or not believe it.

The difficulty is that no option of this second kind can be undecidable on intellectual grounds. That is not true of the first kind. The option – to believe p or not-p – is undecidable on intellectual grounds if there are no better grounds for believing one or the other. It is decidable on intellectual grounds if there are such grounds. Consider now the second sort of option, to believe p or not believe it. It will be undecidable on intellectual grounds if the grounds for believing p and for not believing it are equivalent. But that condition cannot ever be met. The possibilities are these: either there are better reasons for believing p, or there are better reasons for believing not-p, or the reasons are equivalent. In the first case, the option is decidable on intellectual grounds, and in favour of p. In the second case, it is decidable on intellectual grounds, and in favour of not-p. In the third case, where the reasons are equivalent, the option between believing p and not believing it is still decidable on intellectual grounds. The reason is that there are intellectual grounds for suspending judgment, and therefore, for not believing p. It is, then, one and only one kind of option which is undecidable on intellectual grounds, and the other kind, and it only, which is forced. It is a conclusion which makes nonsense of James's thesis statement.

Fortunately, there is a way out of that impasse. What creates the problem is what James says about the meaning of "forced." What clears it up is the recognition that he does not use the word in the way he says he does. There are many indications of that throughout the essay. None is more striking than what he says in the second half of his thesis statement.

It makes two claims. The first is this: to say "Do not decide, but leave the question open" is as much a passional decision as is deciding yes or no. The second is that to say "Do not decide, but leave the question open" is a decision which is attended with the same risk of losing the truth as is deciding yes or no. As they stand, the statements are about saying "leave the question open," not about deciding to leave it open. Saying "Do not decide" is not a decision. It is, therefore, neither a passional nor a non-passional one. For the same reason, it is neither a risky nor a safe one. So, it will be an improvement if we replace James's words by the following: "for deciding to suspend judgment, to leave the question open, is itself a passional decision – just like deciding yes or no – and is attended with the same risk of losing the truth." The claims, then, become, first, that deciding to suspend judgment is as much a passional decision as is deciding yes or no; and second, that deciding to suspend judgment is attended with the same risk of losing the truth as is deciding yes or no.

Both claims are false. When a decision between alternatives cannot be made on intellectual grounds, there are, for that very reason, intellectual grounds for suspending judgment. That does not mean that the decision to leave the question open cannot be a passional one. It does mean, however, that it need not be that. The other claim is at best an understatement of the truth. If I say yes I may be right, and I may be wrong. If I suspend judgment, I cannot be wrong. That is one side of the coin. The other is that I cannot be right either. I run no risk of being wrong, but I do more than just run the risk of losing the truth. I guarantee it. He who sits on the fence cannot be either on the right side of it or on the wrong one. So, the trouble with the second claim is that suspending judgment is attended with more than just the risk of losing the truth. It carries a guarantee of that.

So much for the claims James does make; now for the one he so conspicuously does not make. He is responding to the case for suspending judgment. He denies that it is a way of avoiding passional decisions. He denies that it is a way of avoiding risk. There is another, and crushing response, he might have made. It is that when the option is forced, suspending judgment is strictly impossible. He does not make it. He does not write that to say, under such circumstances, "Do not decide but leave the question open," is to talk nonsense. He advises against leaving the question open, denies that it has the advantages claimed for it. That means he thought it could be done, that there was a possibility of not choosing – under the circumstances, even, that is, when the option is forced. So, his use of the term "forced" does not match his account of his use of it; his profession does not correspond with his practice.

How then does he use it? If something is logically impossible, we cannot do it, but much that we cannot do is logically possible. Often we cannot for lack of ability; often we cannot for lack of opportunity. But what made it impossible for George Washington to tell a lie was neither of these. It was his moral scruples. What prevents many of us from putting all our eggs into one basket is our scruples about acting imprudently, our "prudential scruples." "Cannot" often means "cannot afford to," and despite his own profession, that is what James means by "forced." A forced option is one which we cannot afford not to decide. We can suspend judgment, we can leave the question open, we can avoid deciding it. That is not impossible, but we just cannot afford to do it.[14]

Several things follow. One is that James is not, in the second half of his statement, advising us not to do what, in the first half, he has told us we cannot do anyway. He is advising us against doing what we can, but cannot afford to do. Another is that an option of the kind, to believe p or not-p, can be both forced and undecidable on intellectual grounds. It will be, if we cannot afford to leave it open and yet have no intellectual grounds on which to decide it. So, there is no reason to think that James had in mind an option of any other kind. There are implications, also, for the "must" in "not only lawfully may but must," and for the question how to take that phrase. If we are right about "forced," we must decide a forced option, not because there is no possibility of not choosing; we must decide it in spite of the fact that there is a possibility of not choosing. If so, then what the "must" expresses is not necessity; what it expresses has to be obligation. That obligation is not necessarily the prudential one.

A.C.'s option was a forced one. He could, but could not afford, to leave the question open. His life depended on it. The reasons he could not afford to suspend judgment were prudential ones. The reasons one cannot afford to do something may be moral, not prudential. They were so in George Washington's case. It was not his life, but his moral integrity that was at stake. So, if we have concluded that the doctrine is an ought-to-decide and not just a right-to-decide one, it is still an open question whether the "ought" is the prudential or the moral one, whether the doctrine is a foolish-not-to-decide or a duty-to-decide one.

In short, we have not settled everything. That is as it should be. It would be foolish to decide on the nature of James's claim about religion without consulting section x, the place where that claim is made. We have settled something, however. It is that his thesis statement asserts not just a right but some kind of obligation.

CHAPTER FIVE

Momentous and Intellectually Undecidable Options

An option is forced, we have said, if we cannot afford to leave the question open, if we cannot afford not to decide it. That leaves two things we can afford to do. One is to decide for something, the other is to decide against it. One of these has to be eliminated if the conclusion to be drawn in not just that we must decide the option but that we must decide in favour of something. It is the rôle of James's term "momentous" to do that job. As a forced option is one which we cannot afford not to decide, a momentous option is one which we cannot afford to decide in one of the two ways in which we can decide it. If that is so – and the case will be made – the term "momentous" is no less crucial to his argument than the term "forced." That is also true of the phrase "cannot by its nature be decided on intellectual grounds." The conclusion he wants is not just that we must decide the religious option, and not just that we must decide it in favour of religion. It is, in his idiom, that our passional nature must decide it; in ours, that we must decide it otherwise than on intellectual grounds. That requires the claim that the religious option is undecidable on intellectual grounds. So that claim, also, is a vitally important part of his thesis statement, deserving the same attention as the other parts of it. It also harbours some problems. In short, there are reasons to linger a bit longer in section IV.

James described an option as "the decision between two hypotheses."[1] That cannot be right, for we cannot decide a decision, and we can decide an option. The easy way out of that difficulty – in his phrase, "decide an option between propositions" – is just to drop the word "option" and speak of "deciding between propositions." Later in the sentence, when one does need a noun to which to attach the qualifiers "genuine" and "undecidable on intellectual grounds," "question" will do, or "issue," or anything else that is not a decision but a something-to-be-decided. There is another difficulty which cannot be decided quite so easily, however.

When we decide between propositions, we are deciding, or so it would seem, between statements or assertions or, to use James's preferred term, hypotheses. An hypothesis, he said, was "anything that may be proposed to our belief."[2] In that case, we decide between propositions when we decide what is the case, when we decide, for example, that the dress is blue, not black. It is odd, then, that when James gives examples of different kinds of options, living and dead ones, forced and avoidable ones, momentous and trivial ones, the question in most of them is not what is the case, but what to do.[3] I decide his options, not by coming to believe something, but by acting in some way. Consider the following options; to go out with my umbrella or without it, to love or to hate someone, to accept or decline an invitation to join an expedition. What are the propositions I accept when I decide such options? It is a mistake to think that I decide them by coming to believe that it will rain, or that it will not, that the expedition will succeed, or that it will fail. Suppose I come to believe it will rain. I may still be undecided about what to do with the umbrella. I may even decide against taking it. Suppose I decide the expedition will be an enormous success. I may still remain undecided about whether to accept. I may even decide to decline. On the other hand, I may decide to take the umbrella or not to, to accept the invitation or to decline it, without coming to any belief about the likelihood of rain or the prospects for the expedition. It is not, then, by coming to believe any proposition that I decide these options, but only by performing some action. That makes James's choice of examples rather an odd one. It is not only odd, however; it is more than a little incautious. There is no guarantee that options between actions will serve as models for options between propositions, no guarantee that features belonging to some, at least, of the one will belong to any of the other. James uses the one kind of option as a model for the other, most notably in his account of "momentous." In doing so, he does not avoid all of the pitfalls.

If one got an invitation to join Nansen's expedition, he says, the option would be a momentous one.[4] That is because of the following three things. It would be unique; one is not likely to get another invitation like it. The decision, once taken, would be irreversible; when the expedition has sailed, if I am not on board, I am not one of Nansen's party, however much I may now wish I had said yes and not no. A great deal is at stake; accepting gives me a share in Nansen's chance of immortality, declining cuts me off from that possibility altogether. An option is not momentous, but trivial, if it lacks any of these marks; it is trivial if the opportunity is not unique, trivial if the decision is always reversible, and trivial if nothing much is at stake.

That account of a momentous option is closely modelled on James's example, and the example, as already noted, is not an option between propositions. There, what I have to decide is what to do. Moreover, I have to decide it within a given time. After that, the question no longer arises. That is why my decision will become irreversible. When the expedition has left without me, I cannot change my mind and accept. The invitation has expired. The question what to do about it no longer arises. To go, or not to go, that *was* the question, but is no longer. There is something, however, about which I still can change my mind. Suppose I sent my regrets, having decided that the venture would fail. I cannot change my mind about accepting, but I can change it about the failure of the venture. I can come to think that, despite everything, the venture will succeed. So my decision on that matter is quite reversible. It is not reversible permanently. There is a time when that question, too, no longer arises. It no longer arises when the expedition is complete and safely home. Then, the question "Did it succeed?" may still be asked, but not any more "Will it succeed?" The time for that is over. Some questions, however, seem not to "expire," to be permanent ones, and the religious question is one of these. If it is permanent, there is no reason to think that a decision about it is ever irreversible. In fact, there is good reason to think it is not. Most people have changed their minds about it at least once, and many have changed them oftener than that. It looks like a question on which one can change one's mind as long as one has a mind to change. It is not surprising, then, that when James gets around to claiming that the religious option is a momentous one, there is no more mention of "irreversibility." That condition has been quietly dropped.

One last point before we leave "momentous." It is that a momentous option is one which we cannot afford to decide *against*. We cannot afford to say no to Nansen. His offer is just too good to turn down. There is too much to be gained by saying yes, too much, then, to be lost by saying no. Religion, James is going to say later, makes the very same claim about the religious option.[5] It says that the religious option is a momentous one. The case it makes is that if we decide it positively we gain something better than a share in Nansen's chance of immortality, a certain vital good. We lose that vital good if we decide against. We lose it also if we do not decide. So the total case is that the religious option is both forced and momentous. We cannot afford to leave it undecided, and we cannot afford to decide against it either. If that is so, then, of course, the only way we can afford to deal with the religious option is by deciding for theism.

We can turn now to the other phrase in James's thesis statement, his "cannot by its nature be decided on intellectual grounds." Some questions arise when the phrase is considered just by itself. Of these the principal one is what sorts of grounds are to count as intellectual ones. Some other questions arise when the phrase is considered in relation to the requirements of his argument and the rather different description which he gives of the religious option in section x. Among these are the questions whether "cannot be decided" means "cannot ever be decided" or "cannot yet be decided," and what the relation is between "undecidability on intellectual grounds," the language of section IV, and "scientific unverifiability," the rather different language of section x. These questions are interconnected, answers to some of them depending in part upon answers to others. We can begin, however, with the first one.

The question is whether all grounds are intellectual ones, empirical as well as a priori, or whether only a priori grounds are to count as intellectual ones. The answer is that all grounds are intellectual ones. Of course, if it were James's view that the religious question cannot ever be decided on intellectual grounds, and if it were his hope that sometime it can be decided on empirical or scientific ones, then intellectual grounds would have to be limited to a priori ones. It is very doubtful, however, that James held that the religious option cannot ever be decided on intellectual grounds. Further, it is more than doubtful that in holding some options to be undecidable on intellectual grounds – to be decidable only by our passional nature – he was holding no more than that they are decidable only on empirical ones.

That brings us to the other questions. To advance his argument, James must claim that the religious option is a "genuine" one and one which "cannot by its nature be decided on intellectual grounds." In section x, the term "genuine" does not appear at all, but "forced," "living," and "momentous" all do, and a claim that all three apply to the religious option is tantamount to the claim that it is a "genuine" one. The phrase "cannot by its nature be decided on intellectual grounds" does not appear either, and this time no obvious equivalent is doing duty for it. What is said about the religious hypothesis is that it "cannot yet be verified scientifically at all."[6] That is clearly not an equivalent for the other phrase. There would be nothing unusual or implausible in distinguishing "intellectual" from "scientific," in claiming, for example, that the sphere of the intellect is wider than that of science. There is no reason to think James was drawing that distinction however. The one he does draw in section x is between the head and the heart, not between different intellectual activities. So it would not be out of the question to treat "cannot be verified scientifically" as no more than a stylistic variant for "cannot be decided on intellectual grounds." The problem, obviously, lies elsewhere. It lies in the presence of "yet" in his one phrase and its absence from the other one. Abstractly, there are two ways of bringing the phrases into line. One is to cut "yet" from "cannot yet be verified scientifically at all."[7] The other is to add "yet" to "cannot by its nature be decided on intellectual grounds."

James's argument requires that the two phrases be brought into line, and the better way to do it is to add "yet" to his "cannot by its nature be decided on intellectual grounds." The resulting phrase, "cannot ... yet be decided on intellectual grounds" is all that his conclusion requires. If we do not yet have intellectual grounds on which to decide an option, and if the option is one which we ought to decide (because, among other things, we cannot afford to postpone a decision), his conclusion follows that we ought to decide it and to do so otherwise than on intellectual grounds. Adding "yet" may seem to invite the objection that, if the lack of intellectual grounds is not permanent, what we ought to do is postpone deciding until such time as we have them. That objection is ruled out, however, by the fact that the option is a forced one. The other way of reconciling the two phrases is to cut "yet" from "cannot yet be verified scientifically at all." That would mean ascribing to James the view that the religious hypothesis cannot ever be verified scientifically at all. There is no doubt that many would applaud his holding that view. Religion, they say, is not science, and religious claims cannot be verified scientifically, ever. Many would applaud if not only the "yet" were absent but the "scientifically" also. Religious utterances, they say, are not assertions, can have no truth-value, and, so, cannot be verified, scientifically or otherwise, ever. The question, however, is not whether James should have held these views. It is whether there is any reason to think that he did hold them, whether they are required, for example, by other things he said or even fit with them. The answer is that they are not required, that they do not fit, and that there is reason, therefore, to think he did not hold them.

Consider, first, section x of his essay. It is impossible to read it as ruling out all possibility of verification. The obvious fact is that he is deliberately ruling it in. One striking feature about the passage is the frequent reference to "evidence." In many cases, it is true, he is saying that evidence is not available. In a good many others, however, he is denouncing the folly of doing what will make it permanently unavailable. In particular, he is warning against suspending judgment on the ground that it will do just that. That warning, while it is consistent with the view that religion cannot yet be verified, makes nonsense of the view that it cannot be verified ever. "Yet," in short, has to stay. What of "scientifically"? Unlike "yet," it is hardly worth fighting over. The important question is whether James held the religious option to be one which by its nature cannot yet be decided on intellectual grounds. It is clear, however, and worth adding, that he did not share the view that religious claims cannot be either confirmed or confuted by scientific ones. He remarked that some religious claims had in fact been so confuted.[8] Given that view, it is not surprising at all that he should have thought of the religious hypothesis as something which, one day, would be confirmed by science or confuted by it.

Consider, second, his preface to *The Will to Believe*. At one point in it he describes the scientists' terms for signing a treaty of peace with religion. The terms will allow the religious man to continue enjoying his religious faith on condition that he do it quietly among his friends and not make a public nuisance of it in the market place. James rejects peace bought at such a price, and his reason is decisive for our question. Agreeing to such terms, he says, would abolish the experimental tests by which truth is sifted from falsity in religion. It would do so because it is only the active faiths of individuals in their religious views, freely expressing themselves in life, that are "the experimental tests by which they are verified, and the only means by which their truth or falsehood can be wrought out."[9] To be sure, that leaves many supplementary questions unanswered. But it does one thing. It routs any suggestion that James thought of the religious option as one which could not ever be decided on intellectual grounds.

Consider, finally, the last chapter of *The Principles of Psychology*.[10] It is relevant because it gives in a systematic way James's division of propositions. Its effect is to confirm the message of our other sources, for it gives no hint of the existence of any propositions which cannot ever be verified at all.

The division goes like this. Propositions are first divided into those which are empirical and those which are not.[11] The non-empirical ones are then divided into those which express the results of comparison only, and those which do not.[12] Finally, those which are not based upon comparison only are divided into those "which the world verifies" and those "not as yet so verified."[13] Diagrammatically, it looks like this:

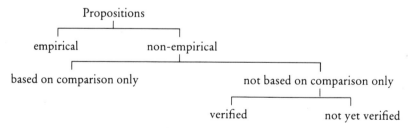

As examples of the class of empirical propositions, James gives such proximate laws of nature as "fire burns," "water wets," "fishes live in water and die on land."[14] The class of non-empirical propositions based only on comparison contains the truths of the pure sciences, including logic and mathematics.[15] Into the class of non-empirical propositions which are not based on comparison only but which are verified, James places the propositions of the natural sciences;[16] and the propositions of metaphysics, together with those of ethics and aesthetics, are put into the class of non-empirical propositions which are not based on comparison only and which are not as yet so verified.[17]

The position expressed in that division requires more clarification than we can engage in here.[18] Its bearing on our question is clear enough, however. If we except the proximate laws of nature, all propositions in his scheme are a priori. So, the propositions of metaphysics, ethics, aesthetics do not differ generically from those of the pure sciences or those of the natural sciences. There are differences, of course. Those of the pure sciences do not need to be verified,[19] those of the natural sciences have already been verified, and those of metaphysics, ethics and aesthetics still await the verification which they require.[20] There is no place, there, for propositions which cannot be verified ever. The religious hypothesis, unverified but requiring verification, will belong with the propositions of metaphysics and those others which cannot yet be verified at all.

We have been concerned so far with the major premise of James's argument, with the thesis statement of section IV. We have sought to clarify the more important of its words and phrases. If we have succeeded in doing that, we have succeeded at the same time in throwing light on both the minor premise of his argument and the conclusion which is entailed. What remains to be done is to see how James supports his minor premise – the claim that the religious option is both genuine and undecidable on intellectual grounds – and how he expresses the conclusion. Our attention shifts now, in short, to section X.

CHAPTER SIX

The Religious Hypothesis

The first question is what the religious option is, and James begins with it, with a definition of religion.[1] He notes that religions vary widely and that a definition must be broad enough to cover them all. The one he gives is put in terms of what religion affirms. It is said to affirm essentially two things. The first is given more than one formulation, but the one finally settled on is the phrase "perfection is eternal." The second is that we are better off even now if we believe that first claim.

Some undeserved ridicule has been directed against James's definition, and especially against its first part.[2] Perhaps it is a mistake to define religion by looking for some feature which is common and peculiar to all religions; perhaps it is another mistake to look for that feature in the area of doctrine, in what religions affirm. If these are mistakes, James makes them, and in good company. There is something, nevertheless, to be said on his side. It has been plausibly argued that the religious attitude presumes an infinite superiority on the part of the religious object, a superiority which includes some kind of necessary or non-contingent existence.[3] If that is so, his "perfection is eternal," and his other formulations also, will seem not so very far off the mark. It has to be kept in mind that what James is after is something "very generic and broad."[4] That explains why his definition does not use the term "God." In *our* religions, he says later, the real "is no longer a mere *It* to us but a *Thou*."[5] That is what makes the term "God" appropriate in an account of *our* religions and inappropriate in a definition of religion.

It is the inclusion of the second affirmation that is the more questionable, the inclusion of the claim that we are better off even now if we believe that first one. What is questionable is not, of course, that religion makes that claim: it is the incorporation of it into the definition. Atheism claims that we are better off if we believe that God does not exist, but one would not include that affirmation in the definition of atheism.

There seems no good reason to do differently with theism. James's argument, further, does not require its inclusion. What it does require is that religion should pose a forced and momentous option. That requirement is met if the first of the two claims does so, and James thinks it does. It is not a requirement that the second should do so also, and he does not so much as raise the question whether it does. We cannot afford not to believe that God exists, he will claim later, but no claim is ever made, or even considered, that we cannot afford not to believe that we are better off believing that perfection is eternal.

To the question why he included that second affirmation, it is easy to guess at an answer. He may well have thought that building it into the definition of religion would serve in place of an argument that the religious option is a forced and momentous one. Saying that we are better off if we believe something is a not too rough equivalent for saying that we cannot afford not to believe it, and the latter is, as we have seen, the claim that the option in question is a forced and momentous one. In effect, then, what James has done is to make religion's second claim the claim that its first one poses a forced and momentous option. The trouble is that doing that does not meet the requirements of his argument. James himself must claim that the religious option is forced and momentous – not just claim that religion claims that it is – and he must support the claim with some sort of reason. In section x, he does claim and argue that the religious option is forced and momentous. The argument turns, how-ever, not on his definition of religion, not even on its first part only, but on his account of our religions.

It was said earlier that his argument is a syllogism, that its major premise is given in the thesis statement of section IV, and that its minor premise and conclusion come in section x. That description, although useful, is, of course, incomplete. It will help fill it out if we consider the following questions.

1 Is the doctrine of section x an ought-to-believe or a right-to-believe one?

2 Is the "ought" or "right" prudential or moral?

3 Given that his premise is about deciding, how can he draw a conclusion about believing?

4 Given that his premise is about deciding, not about deciding for rather than against, how can he conclude, not just that we may and must decide the religious option, but that we must believe theism rather than atheism?

5 If his case is that we are best off believing theism – as his earlier case was that A.C. was best off believing he could make the leap – what reason does he give in section x to support that claim?

The first two questions are the same ones that were asked earlier about his 1875 position in the *Nation*. In effect, then, they ask whether his claim in "The Will to Believe" is continuous with that earlier one. The last is the same question as was asked about his justification of the subjective method. It asks, in effect, whether his argument in "The Will to Believe" is a repetition of that earlier one.

The answer to the first question, as we saw, turns on the meaning of "forced." In section x, as in section iv, James's practice contradicts his profession in section i. He says two things.[6] One is that if the religious claim is false, we avoid error if we suspend judgment. The other is that if the religious claim is true, by suspending judgment we lose a vital good. The obvious implication of both statements is that we *can* suspend judgment, that an option is not forced because we just cannot avoid it: it is forced because avoiding it costs too high a price, because, as we said before, we cannot afford to avoid it. That implication is made quite explicit in his later remark: "Indeed we *may* wait if we will, – I hope you do not think that I am denying that, – but if we do so, we do so at our peril as much as if we believed."[7] His claim in section x, that we not only lawfully may but must decide the religious option, is not the claim that deciding it is permissible because it is unavoidable. It asserts not just a right but an obligation. It is not a "may-because-must" claim, but a "may-indeed-must" one.

The second question turns on the meaning of "lawfully," on the kind of law that is meant. In section x, two things are important. One is the conclusion he draws. The other is the statement, just quoted, in which he denies denying that we may wait if we will. The conclusion he draws is not that suspending judgment is wrong, sinful, the lowest or any other depth of immorality. It is that it is absurd.[8] So the law in question is not moral but prudential. If it is absurd not to believe, that means that prudence requires believing; it means – moving to the other statement – that prudentially it is not the case that we may wait if we will. So his claim that we may wait is not, then, a prudential one. Is it a moral one? The moral challenge to James's foolish-not-to-believe doctrine was the claim that, in the absence of evidence, it is always immoral to believe, even when it is prudent. If James disagreed, as clearly he did, there were two courses open to him. He could say that sometimes there was nothing morally wrong with believing. He could take the stronger line that sometimes there was something morally wrong with not believing, with suspending judgment. That would be to assert a moral duty to believe, to say that we morally must do it. There is no evidence in his essay that he took that stronger line. What he concludes about suspending judgment is not that it is immoral, but that sometimes it is absurd. When he proposes that both sides cease issuing vetoes to one another,[9] he is rejecting alike the duty-not-to-believe and the duty-to-believe doctrines. He is saying that morally speaking we may believe, and, also, that we may refrain. In short, when he says that we lawfully may and must believe, the "may" is both prudential and moral, the "must" prudential only. When he says that we may wait if we will, the "may" is moral, and moral only. The case against suspending judgment is that sometimes it is unwise, not that it is immoral.

The answer to the third question is that James attempts no justification at all for the move from "deciding an option between propositions" to "believing." The question whether "believe" is the right word in his title, whether his essay is about belief at all, will be taken up later. Anything that needs to be added can wait until then.

About the fourth question; the defence of religion requires more, obviously, than the claim that we may and must decide the religious option. That excludes agnosticism, but it leaves atheism as much in place as theism. The claim that it is foolish not to believe does more. It rejects disbelieving as well as suspending judgment. The case James makes in section x is, as we shall see presently, an argument for the second of those claims, not just for the first one. It finds the same fault in denial as in doubt.

It is the last of our questions that is the crucial one, and it cannot be answered so quickly. James's treatment of it consists of two parts. The first is an examination of the case for suspending judgment. It proceeds on the assumption that religion is the affirmation that perfection is eternal. The second supplies the reason why we are best off believing. It proceeds on the basis of a new definition of religion, or rather, on the basis of a new definition of *our* religions.

What can be said for suspending judgment is that it is a guarantee against believing incorrectly. What can be said against it is that it is no less a guarantee against believing correctly. Belief has neither of those guarantees, but it has its own advantages and disadvantages. If we believe, we may be right, but we may also be wrong. To suspend judgment is, thus, to trade the chance of being right for the guarantee of not being wrong. To believe is to trade the guarantee of not being wrong for the chance of being right. Either trade may be a good one or a bad one. If I suspend judgment about p, I cannot be mistaken about it. But it can be a mistake to suspend judgment about it. It will be a mistake if p is true and if I should otherwise have believed it. It will be no mistake if p is false and if I should otherwise have believed it. In the one case I have traded the best for the second best; in the other, the worst for the second best.

That suspending judgment does not avoid all risks is one of the points James is anxious to make. In the passage already quoted, he said that if we wait "we do so at our peril as much as if we believed."[10] The second point he is anxious to make is that, without knowing whether p is true or false, there is no way of knowing which of the two trades is the better one. "Dupery for dupery, what proof is there," he asks, "that dupery through hope is so much worse than dupery through fear? I, for one, can see no proof."[11] Those two points do not exhaust the thrust of his argument, however. They show that those who advocate suspending judgment are in no better position to be giving advice than anyone else. They do nothing to show that the advice they give is bad advice. The second part of the argument is designed to show that that is so, in some cases at least.

There are two distinct cases where he is prepared to argue it. One is when the belief is self-verifying. The other is when evidence about p can be had only if p is first believed. In the first case, believing p makes for the truth of p, so, if I want p to be true, I am well-advised to believe it. In the other case, believing p helps us discover whether p is true or not, so, if I want evidence about p, I am well-advised to believe it. If there really are cases of that second sort – where we can get evidence about p only if we first believe it – it *will* be illogical, absurd, to suspend judgment and keep looking for evidence. Suspending judgment will ensure that evidence is never found, and James will be right in branding as folly the advice to do that. He will be right to denounce that advice when it is given about the religious option, provided that *it* is a case of that sort. He gives no argument that it is, at least not yet. What he does now is to add to the two-part definition of religion a third part, not for the purpose of correcting any defect in the earlier one, but to make the account less "generic and broad." The result is that the new account will fit, not all religions, but rather, all *our* religions.

That third affirmation is that the perfect, the eternal is personal, and that evidence about it is attainable only on condition that we first believe. That paraphrase, it must be granted, is a bit more forthright than the language James uses. It is not a distortion, however. That hardly needs saying about the first part of it. "The more perfect and more eternal aspect of the universe," he wrote, "is represented in our religions as having personal form. The universe is no longer a mere *It* to us, but a *Thou*, if we are religious ... "[12] The rest of our paraphrase relies on his remark about our religions' appealing "to our own active good will, as if evidence might be forever withheld from us unless we met the hypothesis half-way";[13] and on his further one about our feeling that "one who should shut himself up in snarling logicality ... might cut himself off forever from his only opportunity of making the gods' acquaintance."[14] The same lack of forthrightness marks the expression of his conclusion. It is that if religion were true in all its three branches, "pure intellectualism, with its veto on our making willing advances, would be an absurdity."[15] What that language leaves in no doubt whatsoever is that the charge against agnosticism is one of absurdity, illogicality, not one of immorality. What admittedly it leaves less clear is that it is belief he is talking about. "Meeting the hypothesis half-way," "making willing advances" are not, on the face of them, or in all contexts, equivalents for believing. In the present context, however, where the argument is for the absurdity of suspending judgment, of not believing, it is hard to see how they can be taken otherwise.

If that is James's argument, it helps clear up some earlier problems. It means that what he built into his account of *our* religions is not quite the claim that the religious option is undecidable on intellectual grounds, but something quite like that. What he is saying about the religious hypothesis is that we cannot have evidence about it unless we first believe it, that we have, therefore, to accept it not on evidence – if we accept it at all – and that only if we do accept it do we have any chance of getting evidence, of having an intellectual ground for retaining the belief or discarding it. Saying that is something like saying that it cannot be decided on intellectual grounds. It is saying that initially it cannot be so decided. The difference is that it does acknowledge that belief may *subsequently* be based on intellectual grounds – and disbelief too. The best way, perhaps, of expressing the position would be to insert "yet" into his "cannot by its nature be decided on intellectual grounds" – a move which has already been suggested for other reasons. "Yet" will then mean, in part, "in advance of believing." In short, James's trouble is not, as some have thought it is, that he sometimes slipped in "yet" where it did not belong.[16] The trouble is that he sometimes left it out where it did belong.

The argument helps, also, with a second problem. It was noted earlier that James's conclusion does not match his premise. He concludes that we are unwise not only to leave the option undecided, but also to decide for the negative side. He concludes further, not just that we may and must decide for religion, but that we may and must believe it. No case is ever given for the second of these claims – for the move from deciding to believing – but there is support for the other one in the argument we have been considering. There, it is not only if we leave the option undecided that we cut ourselves off from the chance of getting evidence. We do that, also, if we come down on the negative side. It is foolish, therefore, not to decide, and foolish, also, to decide against religion. That is not, or not only, because we lose the emotive and conative benefits that accrue from deciding for religion. It is because we lose the cognitive benefit. Only if we first decide, groundlessly, for religion – the claim is – do we have any chance of later getting grounds, any chance of later deciding about it rationally. So, Santayana was preaching to the converted when he reproached James; "Believe, certainly; we cannot help believing; but believe rationally ... "[17] James was already agreed. He wanted to believe rationally. He wanted to believe rationally even in those cases where, as it seemed to him, one could not, without believing, get evidence on which to believe rationally.

James's claim in "The Will to Believe" is, then, continuous with the one announced in 1875 in the *Nation*. It is an ought-to-believe doctrine, not a right-to-believe one, and the "ought" is prudential, not moral. Just like the other, it is a foolish-not-to-believe doctrine. Built into it, in a subordinate position, is a moral right-to-believe thesis, a rejection of the duty-not-to-believe thesis of Clifford and Huxley. In the early papers, the main thesis is supported by an argument which turns on the claim that some beliefs are self-verifying. When believing makes it so, it is foolish not to believe what you want to be true. In "The Will to Believe," no claim is made that religious belief is self-verifying.[18] In it the supporting argument turns on the different claim that there are cases where we cannot have evidence about a proposition unless we first believe it.[19] That is, of course, a highly paradoxical claim, in itself strange enough to prompt the question which will concern us in the following chapters, the question whether "believe" is really the right word.

CHAPTER SEVEN

Belief and Other Things

James, as we have seen, had second thoughts about his title for "The Will to Believe." He would have done better, he thought, if he had written "Right" rather than "Will." Apparently, he had no second thoughts about the word "Believe." It remained in place in the alternative formulation which he came to prefer. Nevertheless, the question whether James's essay is really about belief is not a frivolous one. There is a case to be made that "believe," also, is not the right word. There are, at least, two arguments which lead quickly to that conclusion. One turns on the premise that to believe is to believe on evidence. The other turns on the premise that expressions like "God exists" are not propositions. Both premises entail that the essay cannot be about belief, and both of them command a following.

It is clear how the arguments will go. Suppose – to begin with the first one – that to believe is to believe on evidence. Then, to put it paradoxically, to believe not on evidence is not to believe. It does not follow, of course, that one cannot decide an option between propositions otherwise than on evidence, otherwise than on intellectual grounds. It does follow that so to decide it is not to believe. In short, if James's essay is about deciding otherwise than on intellectual grounds, then – the argument is – it cannot be about belief, and "believe" is certainly the wrong word in his title.

The crucial claim in that argument, the premise that to believe is to believe on evidence, has appealed to a good many philosophers. One of them puts it this way.[1] To believe p is to estimate that p is more probable than not; to estimate that p is more probable than not is to claim a balance of evidence in favour of p; so, to believe p is to claim a balance of evidence in favour of p. If he is right, "believe" has to be the wrong word in James's essay just because it is about deciding between propositions in the absence of any claimed balance of evidence, in the absence of intellectual grounds.

The argument is not convincing, however. Its crucial claim is that one cannot estimate that p is more probable than not, except on the basis of a balance of evidence. The truth is, rather, that without such a basis, the probability estimate will be groundless, but not that it cannot be made. In that case, belief which fails to pass the evidential test is still belief. It is just groundless belief. It is true, further, that when it becomes apparent that a belief was groundless, we sometimes say, not that we believed p, but that we took it for granted.[2] The conclusion sometimes drawn is that belief is not belief unless it is grounded. The inference, once again, is unwarranted. The fact does not show that when belief is groundless we consider "belief" to be the wrong word, a mistaken word. It shows only that we consider "take for granted" to be a better one. In short, this first argument that James's essay cannot be about belief, is an invalid one, for the crucial claim is false which it makes about the nature of belief.

The premise of our second argument is, to put it paradoxically, that religious propositions are not propositions. Its impact on James's case is direct and clear. Where there are no propositions, there are no options between propositions, and no deciding of options between propositions. No principle about deciding options between propositions can apply, then, in the case of religion. If there are no religious propositions, but only pseudo-propositions, it follows that there are no religious beliefs, but only religious pseudo-beliefs – assuming, that is, that to believe is to believe a proposition. A good many philosophers endorse the view that religious propositions are pseudo-propositions. They express it sometimes in the catch-phrase, "religion without propositions." Not all of them embrace the consequence that religious belief is not belief but pseudo-belief, preferring to retain the term "belief" and to redefine it.[3] But the consequence is clear that, if religious propositions are not propositions, religious belief is not belief, if belief is belief in a proposition.

What lies behind the expression, "religion without propositions," is the view that nothing is a proposition unless it meets a certain criterion, expressed commonly as "falsifiability in principle."[4] Nothing, in short, is a proposition unless there is some conceivable state of affairs which it rules out, and some conceivable state of affairs, therefore, which, if it were to be actual, would falsify it. That is combined with the claim that religious utterances are not so falsifiable. James, it is fairly clear, would not agree. Religious propositions, in his view, *are* propositions, and they are falsifiable in principle. There are, certainly, places where he seems to say something different. He describes some options between propositions as by their nature undecidable on intellectual grounds, and that description invites the comment that they are not, then, options between propositions. He implies, also, that the religious option is one such option. He does, however, as we have seen, warn against doing what will cut us off from ever getting evidence which would confirm or confute the religious claim; and the extent of the claim which he makes about religion is that it "cannot yet be verified scientifically at all." That is very different from saying that it "cannot by its nature be decided on intellectual grounds." It is, on the contrary, to suggest that it is in principle so decidable, although in practice not yet.

If these arguments provide no direct route to the conclusion that "believe" is the wrong word in James's title, it may still be that a longer, more circuitous route will take us there. At the heart of that case will be the following claims: first, that James called "belief" some things which are not belief; and second, that his essay reads better if it is read as a justification, not of belief, but of one of those other things. What follows is a presentation of that case. It is a case which is hinted at by one of the quite striking facts about James's essay, the fact that he remained quite unmoved by the extensive and vigorous criticism to which he saw it subjected. Clearly, there was intelligence of high order on both sides of the debate, so it is hard to put the continuing disagreement down to simple lack of comprehension. No doubt one could explain it by appealing to the fact, which James himself insisted upon, that it is not logic alone which settles the creeds of any one of us. There are grounds, however, for suspecting that there is more to it than that. James's critics insist that his essay is not a vindication of belief. They also concede, or some of them do, that it may well be a vindication of something else, something confusable – but, in their view, not to be confused – with belief; and they make different suggestions about what that other thing is.[5] To James, it still seems a powerful vindication of something he calls "belief," and he is, therefore, unimpressed by the objections. Perhaps the reason for that is his own extended, indeed overextended, use of the term "belief." It would seem to be a question well worth asking.

If James's essay is about belief, two things are immediately striking. One is that the word "believe" is conspicuously absent from the passage in which he introduces us to his "thesis." There, as we know, what he says we may and must do is "decide an option between propositions," and the word "believe" does not occur at all. If the argument is a syllogism, the second striking thing is that the language of the premise does not reappear in any of the several versions of the conclusion. There, the term "believe" does occur, however. In other words, the argument's premise is expressed in terms of deciding between propositions, not believing, while its conclusion is expressed in terms sometimes of believing, never of deciding between propositions. In that case, the argument needs to be rescued, and, of course, the simple way of doing that is to take it that the two expressions are being used in it as synonyms.

That still leaves us with a decision to make, however. Two accounts of the essay remain possible. One is that it is really about deciding between propositions and that the word "believe" is being used in it in an abnormally wide way. The other is that it is really about believing, and that the expression, "decide between propositions," is being used in an abnormally restricted way. Putting the matter thus does assume, of course, that in their normal uses, the two expressions are not synonyms, and that the one expression is wider than the other.

It is an assumption not too hard to justify. It was said earlier that when we have come to believe this rather than that, it is a natural enough way of speaking to say that we have decided between two propositions. We do use the word "decide"; we say that we have decided that the dress is blue, not black. It is not, however, only by coming to believe one or the other that we decide between propositions. To decide between propositions is to decide which one to   , and the blank can be filled by any one of several different verbs. Which of them is the appropriate one will depend on the option, the question. For the investigator, for example, the question is which proposition to take as his working hypothesis – that there was foul play or that the death was due entirely to natural causes. For the gambler, the question is different: it is which proposition to take a chance on – that Plato will win the two-thirty, or that Aristotle will. To decide an option between propositions may be, then, to come to believe one of them. It may not be that, however, but rather to adopt this one rather than that as one's working hypothesis; or, to take a chance on this one rather than that. That list of possibilities is not exhaustive. It does make the point, however, that if to believe is to decide between propositions, to decide between propositions is not necessarily to believe; and so, that in their normal senses, these expressions are not synonymous ones.

It is a proper question, then, whether James's essay is about deciding between propositions or about believing. His own answer is that it is about believing. That is clear both from his title and from his frequent use of the word "believe" in statements of his position. He writes of it as the "freedom to believe,"[6] the "freedom to believe what we will,"[7] and the "right to believe at our own risk any hypothesis that is live enough to tempt our will."[8] The question is not about his answer, however, but about ours, and about what should govern it. Suppose that James never expressed his position in any language but that just quoted, that he wrote always of "belief" or used words which clearly were equivalents for it. There would then be no reason at all to depart from his answer. Suppose, however, that he sometimes stated his position in a quite different language, one clearly not synonymous with "belief"; suppose, for example, that he concluded sometimes that we may and must take a chance on theism, gamble on it; or that we may and must take theism as our working hypothesis. Then we should have to give the different answer, to say that his essay was about, not belief, but the wider notion of deciding between propositions.

It is the second of these suppositions that is the correct one. The fact is that James expresses his conclusion in a variety of ways, sometimes in terms of believing theism, sometimes in terms of betting, gambling on it, and sometimes in terms of taking it as one's hypothesis. We have sufficiently noted the first kind of formulation. The important thing now is to notice the others.

In his discussion of Pascal's wager, James remarked that we "probably feel that when religious faith expresses itself thus, in the language of the gaming-table, it is put to its last trumps."[9] He neither affirms there, nor denies, that he himself finds the language inappropriate. It would seem, however, that he does not. He shows no hesitation in using it himself. This, for example, is how he contrasts the sceptic and the believer. "He [the faith-vetoer] is actively playing his stake as much as the believer is; he is backing the field against the religious hypothesis, just as the believer is backing the religious hypothesis against the field."[10] If anything is, that is the language of the gaming-table. The believer is the gambler, and the non-believer is too. That description confirms the suspicion aroused every time James ties together – as he frequently does – the notions of belief and risk. The suspicion is that, although the word used is "believe", what he is talking about is gamble, wager, betting, not believing a proposition, but simply taking a chance on it.

Earlier, we noted a quite different language in which James expressed his position. The case, as we saw him put it then, was for "making willing advances," for not hesitating to meet "the religious hypothesis half-way." It is not, of course, crystal clear what these expressions amount to. It depends on what the limits, the reference points, are. Take them to be acceptance and rejection, and the mid-point between them is suspension of judgment. But James is not advocating suspension of judgment: he is combatting "pure intellectualism" with its advocacy of that. The limits, then, are suspension of judgment and acceptance. In that case, meeting half-way will be something more positive than just keeping an open mind, but less positive than acceptance. It will be something like the state of being "inclined to think," provided we take that expression not for a weak form of belief but, literally, for the state of being "tilted towards believing." Or, it will be like the state of being "tempted to believe," without, however, having yet succumbed to the temptation. It will not be exactly like those, however, for making willing advances is doing something, not a state, but an activity. The most plausible equivalent will be taking a proposition as a matter for active inquiry. More than just keeping an open mind about it and less than outright acceptance, meeting the religious hypothesis half-way, making willing advances towards it, will be acceptance of it as an hypothesis. The reason which James gives for going out to meet the religious hypothesis half-way is that, if we do not, "evidence might be forever withheld from us."[11] In his other, more dramatic language, it is that we may lose our "only opportunity of making the gods' acquaintance."[12] That fits the account just suggested, for it is a truism that we may miss evidence about a proposition if we do not actively inquire.

There is one more term in which James commonly put his position. It is the term, "faith." It occurs, perhaps, as often as "belief" does, more often, certainly, than the others that have been listed. It appears in two of the other titles which he thought preferable to the actual one, although not in his favourite title for the essay. These others are, "A Defense of Faith"[13] and "A Critique of Pure Faith."[14] It is not only in the titles, however, that the words "belief" and "faith" interchange with one another. They do so throughout the body of the paper. At the beginning he calls his essay a "justification of *faith*," and, in apposition, "a defence of our right to adopt a *believing* attitude in religious matters."[15] He remarks, also, that he has long defended "the lawfulness of voluntarily adopted *faith*," having just announced that "'The Will to Believe', accordingly, is the title of my paper."[16] The same pattern persists to the end. "The whole defence of religious *faith*," he says there, "hinges upon action" because "*belief* is measured by action."[17] When he pokes fun at the schoolboy's definition of faith – "when you *believe* something that you know ain't true"[18] – the laugh comes not until the end. There is nothing funny, for James, in defining faith as believing. It is not suggested, of course, that there is anything unusual in that interchanging of "belief" and "faith." It is standard practice among writers on religion. It does mean, however, that in looking at what James says about belief, we cannot ignore what he has to say about faith.

In sum, we have a range of terms which James used in stating his position. They are not, on the face of them, all equivalents, merely different terms for one and the same thing. So the question remains what it is that James's essay is really about. He said it was about belief. A safer answer is that it is about deciding between propositions. The trouble with that answer is that it buys safety at the cost of concreteness. It would be nice to be able to pin things down a bit more precisely. Of course, that may not be possible; but it would seem, at least, to be worth a try.

CHAPTER EIGHT

Belief and Faith

James said his essay was about belief. He said, also, that it was about faith, and used these words interchangeably. If they are not interchangeable and we have to choose between them, it may be that the better way to read his essay is to read it as an essay on faith. Faith, notoriously, is a word of many meanings. Our first question, then, is whether saying that the essay is about faith adds any new candidates to the list we already have.

In what looks like a clear attempt at definition, James wrote as follows: "Faith means belief in something concerning which doubt is still theoretically possible; and as the test of belief is willingness to act, one may say that faith is the readiness to act in a cause the prosperous issue of which is not certified to us in advance."[1] There, the first part looks like a definition of faith, and the last part seems meant as an alternative formulation of it. If so, the claim is that faith may be defined either as belief in something about which doubt is still theoretically possible or, equivalently, as readiness to act in a cause the prosperous issue of which is not certified to us in advance. James moves from the one formulation to the other by substituting, in part, "readiness to act" for "belief." That makes it odd that the claim he makes is not that belief *is* readiness to act, but that the test of belief is willingness to act. Obviously it is the other claim that is needed to warrant the substitution. If belief is readiness to act, the alternative definition will be readiness to act on something concerning which doubt is still theoretically possible. If it is not, we shall have two different things both of which James calls faith. One is believing something which is dubitable. The other is readiness to act on something which is dubitable.

The move from James's first to his second formulation involves another substitution. This other one is justified only if action on something which is dubitable is the same as action in a cause the success of which is not certified to us in advance. These, obviously, are not the same. It is one thing to act on p where p is dubitable and quite another to act to bring it about that p, where success is dubitable. We have, in short, at least two things which James calls faith, and, if belief is different from readiness to act, as many as four. They are:

1 believing what is dubitable,
2 readiness to act on what is dubitable,
3 believing in a cause the success of which is dubitable,
4 readiness to act in a cause the success of which is dubitable.

A curious thing is now worth noting. James commonly described his opponents as vetoers of faith, and himself as its champion and defender. If faith is any of the things just listed, however, it is not in the least controversial, not anywhere under attack, and in no need of a champion. If it is believing what is unsupported by any balance of evidence, it may well be criticized. It may be complained that the thing to do in that case is suspend judgment. Yet no one complains about believing what is dubitable if the evidence favours it, makes it probable. If it is belief in causes which have little chance of success, again it may be criticized. The wisdom of believing in such causes may well be questioned. No one, however, vetoes belief in causes where success is dubitable but probable. Substitute "readiness to act" for "belief" and the same is true. No one condemns readiness to act on propositions which are probable but less than certain: no one condemns readiness to act in causes which are likely but not certain to succeed. On any of these views of faith, it just is nonsense to present the issue between James and his opponents as the question of the lawfulness of faith. That is not to say that James does not do it. He does it often. He does it, for example, at the end of his paper on the subjective method when he ascribes to his opponents a "veto ridicule" against working for causes which are not certain to succeed.[2] Such a veto is ridiculous, but so is the charge that his opponents make it. In other parts of the paper we are in closer touch with reality. In places, as we have seen, he is defending, or proposing to defend, belief in something to which the evidence is unfavourable. In others, he is defending belief in something for which there is no balance of evidence either way. In these cases, belief *is* controversial. We keep the issue a genuine one, then, if we replace "dubitable" by "not likely to be true" or "not likely to succeed."[3] Our four earlier formulations now become

1 believing what is not likely to be true,
2 readiness to act on what is not likely to be true,
3 believing in a cause which is not likely to succeed,
4 readiness to act in a cause which is not likely to succeed.

There are places where James gives a definition of faith which is different from any of these. "Faith is synonymous with working hypothesis,"[4] he says. "Au résumé," he also says, "*foi* et *working hypothesis* sont ici la même chose. Avec le temps la verité se dévoilera."[5] Defining faith as working hypothesis looks like a shrewd debating tactic. Making and testing hypotheses is so much a part of scientific inquiry that no scientist can be opposed to it, at least in principle. That does not mean that he cannot be opposed to a particular hypothesis. He can, and on a variety of grounds. So the identification of faith with working hypothesis is not quite a royal road to the legitimation of faith, even if it is a promising start. It was not for merely tactical reasons, however, that James said what he did. He was persuaded that the similarities between religious creed and scientific hypothesis were real and important and the statements just quoted were meant to dramatize them. The objector will stress the difference. The religious person, he will say, believes his creed; the scientific inquirer does not believe his hypothesis; therefore, faith and working hypothesis are different things. If that is right and James is mistaken, it will be worth inquiring how the mistake arises, and we shall do so shortly. For the present, we add this further account of faith to our four earlier ones. When we combine this list of five with our earlier list of things that James's essay might be about, we have one duplicate and two obviously impossible candidates. The one which appears twice is hypothesizing. The obviously impossible candidates are "belief in a cause" and "readiness to act in a cause." What makes them impossible is that God's existence is not a cause, not something our believing in or acting on can do anything to bring about. When the list is revised, we are left with the following contenders: (1) believing theism; (2) gambling on theism; (3) taking theism as a working hypothesis, and (4) deciding to act on theism. These are not, on the face of them at least, equivalents. To say which one of them the essay is really about, we need to find some reason for preferring one of them to the others. Of course, it may be that there is no one thing that the essay is about, but only different things that different parts of it are about. In that case, it will be of interest to find out why James thought it was about one thing, and why he thought that was belief. It will help if we return to our topic of a moment ago, James's claim about faith and working hypothesis.

A scientific inquirer need not, but may believe his hypothesis. If confirming evidence comes in, he may exclaim that he was sure of it all along. On the other hand, he may be genuinely surprised. If he does believe it, he may be asked why he still calls it an hypothesis. One answer is that, although he does believe it, the evidence to date is not enough to warrant his belief. The inquiry, therefore, continues; the search for adequate evidence goes on. Another answer is that the evidence to date, while adequate to justify present belief, falls short of putting the matter beyond all possible doubt. In that case, too, the inquiry continues, now as a search for evidence that is conclusive. If an inquirer does believe his hypothesis, we can say of him all of the four things which follow. The first two of them can be said because what he believes is an hypothesis. The other two can be said because he believes it.

1 He concedes that his hypothesis is not yet known to be true and that doubt about it is still possible.
2 He concedes that the evidence which he seeks, if it comes at all, will come only in the future, and that when it does come, it may confute rather than confirm.
3 He expects, however, that the evidence to come will confirm his hypothesis, not confute it.
4 In the meantime, believing it and believing that the future will confirm it, he acts as if it were true.

There is a reason for making that list. James's claims that faith and working hypothesis are synonymous are not isolated aphorisms. Both occur in contexts meant to justify them. They do so by stressing similarities between faith and its creed and the scientific inquirer and his hypothesis. What is noteworthy, however, is that the description given of faith resembles only partially the scientific inquirer simpliciter, but duplicates point by point the account just given of the inquirer who believes his hypothesis. The quotations which follow will make the point:

1 "... no non-papal believer at the present day pretends his faith to be of an essentially different complexion [from the hypothesizing of the scientist]; he can always doubt his creed."[6]
2 "... foi et working hypothesis sont ici la même chose. Avec le temps la verité se dévoilera."[7] "His corroboration or repudiation by the nature of things may be deferred until the day of judgment."[8]
3 "The uttermost he now means is something like this: 'I expect then to triumph with tenfold glory.'"[9]
4 "But his intimate persuasion is that the odds in its favour are strong enough to warrant him in acting all along on the assumption of its truth."[10]

The last two of these do not apply to the inquirer simpliciter. He does not expect his hypothesis to be confirmed. At most, he expects the inquiry either to confirm or to confute it, not to show that it is true, but to show whether it is true. Further, he does not, by inquiring, act as if his hypothesis were true. By inquiring, he acts as if it were not yet settled whether it is true or not; he acts as if that question were still an open one. Any resemblance James has shown, then, is between, not faith and hypothesis, but faith and the inquirer who believes his hypothesis. That leads one to ask why he misdescribed the scientific inquirer as he did, describing, in his place, the inquirer who is also a believer. Part of the answer may be that something of the sort was necessary if the thesis he was advancing was to have any plausibility at all. The fact is that there is more to the answer than that, that his reason is a theoretical, not just a practical one. To find it, we have to go to his account of belief.

There are two ways, James said, of studying a psychic state. One is "the way of analysis," the other "the way of history."[11] The first aims at a definition, a statement of the components which together make it up. The other aims at a genetic account, a statement of its antecedent conditions and of its consequences also. Very early, James says that there is nothing to be said about belief on the first score. The fact is that it is indefinable. It is something "perfectly distinct, but perfectly indescribable in words," "a state of consciousness *sui generis*, about which nothing more can be said in the way of internal analysis."[12] If so, then all we can do with belief is history, and history is what the rest of the chapter is meant to be. There are, it is true, places where he seems to take a different view, to hold that belief is definable, that what is wrong with existing definitions of it is that they are partial only, and that the particular merit of his own one is its completeness.[13] These appearances are deceptive, however. What he claims to be giving more completely is not a definition of belief but a history of it.

What bears on our present topic is part of that history, James's position that belief is measured by readiness to act. It makes two claims. One is that no one believes a proposition who is not ready to act on it. The other, the critical one, is that anyone who is ready to act on a proposition also believes it. It is a position which underlies a good deal in James's essay, and it surfaces fairly frequently. It surfaces in his remark that the liveness or deadness – the believability – of an hypothesis is measured by our willingness to act on it.[14] It does so again in his claim that an inquirer's belief in his hypothesis is measured by his willingness to act on it.[15] It is best seen in the opening sentence of one of his footnotes. "Since belief is measured by action, he who forbids us to believe religion to be true, necessarily also forbids us to act as we should if we did believe it to be true."[16] The most striking thing about that remark is its obvious falsity. What it claims is that no one can act on theism who does not believe it, that believing it is a necessary condition of acting on it, that anyone who does act on it, therefore, necessarily also believes it. The other striking thing is its critical importance. James says that the inquirer acts on his hypothesis. In that case, he is bound to say that he also believes it. The view that belief is measured by readiness to act is, in short, the theoretical reason for James's holding that there is no inquirer who is not also a believer.

It has other consequences, too. The gambler acts on the proposition he takes a chance on. In his case, also, then, James is bound to say that he believes. If the gambler denies that – as well he may – if he says it was pure gamble, that he just took a chance on it, James is bound to say he is wrong, just as he is bound to say that the inquirer is wrong who says that, the evidence being not yet in, he does not either believe or disbelieve his hypothesis. James is obviously wrong in both cases, but the point to be stressed, perhaps, is rather this one. We can now see why he remained convinced that his essay was about belief. If it was about any one of the other things on our list, in his view it was also about belief. If there is not any one of them that the essay as a whole is about, but different parts of it are about different ones, then the essay is still about belief. The same thing follows more directly if readiness to act *is* faith, not just the measure or test of it, and if faith is belief. Then the inquirer is a believer, and the gambler is, too. James, as we noted, did say that faith is readiness to act, but the remark looks like a slip, so the case is better argued the other way.

If one question has been answered, another one remains. We have seen why James held his essay was about belief. We have said, too, that his reason was mistaken. That leaves still open the question whether it is about belief or not. One can, of course, say that what a paper is about is what its author says it is about. In that case, James's paper is a justification for believing theism, and the only question is whether the case it gives is a sound case for that position. A good many critics have argued that it is not at all a sound case for that position. They may be right. If they are, it is still worth asking whether the essay does not make a sound case for something. There may be no such thing. If there is, but it is trivial, the poor opinion of the paper will remain in place. If it is not trivial, however, and especially if it is something that the religious person might recognize as faith, there will be more to be said for the paper than has usually been said. We shall come to that question at the end, after we have done some beating about in the neighbouring fields.[17]

James and Some Others

CHAPTER NINE

Clifford

It is widely held that Clifford's "The Ethics of Belief" is the foil for James's will-to-believe doctrine, that his papers on that subject are best illumined when read against the background of Clifford's own essay.[1] The claim is not more than a half-truth and perhaps less. The reason is this. Clifford's paper, unlike James's one, is admirably well named. It is about ethics, about duty. It is an ought-not-to-believe doctrine and the "ought" is unquestionably moral. Further, it is about belief and belief only, not about deciding to act, not about guessing or gambling, not about taking something as an hypothesis. Clifford's paper will illumine James's one, then, only if and in so far as it also is about ethics and about belief. In some measure it *is* about these things. That is what makes the claim a half-truth, not a total untruth. To the extent, however, that James's paper is about prudence, not ethics, and to the extent that it is about things other than belief, the light thrown on it by Clifford's paper will be a distorting, a concealing rather than a revealing one. The rival claim that the real foil for James's doctrine is Pascal's wager is less than a whole truth but more than just a half-truth. Like James's essay, Pascal's pensée is about prudence. Like James's essay, it is not obviously about belief. Our present topic is Clifford, however, not Pascal; so, let us assume now only that two half-truths are better than one, than either one.

Clifford's thesis is that "it is wrong, always, everywhere, and for anyone, to believe anything upon insufficient evidence."[2] Put otherwise, it is that when the evidence is insufficient, one's moral duty is to suspend judgment and go on inquiring. The thesis is introduced by two stories. They are not alike in all respects, but the second adds nothing of importance to the first one. That one is about a shipowner who stifles his doubts about the seaworthiness of his vessel. He lets her sail; she goes down with all lives lost; and he recovers his losses from the insurance company. Clifford's verdict is that what the shipowner did was wrong.

He is right. Suppose, he adds, that the belief, reached by attending to favourable evidence and by averting attention away from unfavourable evidence, is nevertheless, genuinely held. The verdict, he thinks, still stands that what was done was wrong. He is right about that too. His example is quite a complex one, however. The shipowner did believe on insufficient evidence. That is one, but only one feature of his case. Another is that his belief was false. Another is that he acted on his belief. Still another is that his action had profound consequences for other people. That means that three questions need to be asked: what if the belief had been true?; what if the belief had not been acted upon?; and what if the belief is one which has no consequences for other people, either because it is not acted on, or despite the fact that it is?

It is a plausible claim that if the belief had been true, what the shipowner did would still have been wrong. No one would have died. He would not have been "verily guilty of the death of those men."[3] He would, however, have been guilty of gambling with human lives. If, however, while believing his vessel seaworthy, he had not acted on that belief, or, if the belief were one devoid of consequences for other people, it is not clear that there would be anything wrong, even given that it was belief on insufficient evidence. Clifford tries to exclude such cases. One does not believe, he argues, unless one does act when the occasion for so doing arises. No belief, he argues also, is devoid of consequences for other people. It is far from clear, however, that he is right in either of those claims.

He does give the appearance of allowing our second question; what if the belief had not been acted upon? In fact, however, he disallows it. He does so on the ground that a belief not acted on is no belief. He concedes that a belief may not be realized immediately in open deeds. He concedes, also, that a belief may never be exhibited in outward acts if the occasion for so exhibiting it should never arise. No one, however, believes p who is not ready to act on it when the occasion does arise. Had the shipowner ordered an inquiry, then, and not let his vessel sail, that would simply have shown that he did not believe she was sound. In that, however, Clifford is just mistaken. The fact is that one can believe that p while also checking to make sure.

What Clifford does allow is a different question, namely this one: given that he did act on his belief, was what he did wrong for one reason only, that he acted on it, or was it wrong both for that reason and for the reason also that he believed on insufficient evidence? The answer required by his thesis is that it was wrong for both reasons, and that is the one he gives. He also argues for it. In doing so, he agrees that, while believing the ship was sound, he still could have called for an inquiry. He adds, however, that anyone who already believes p, or even wishes to, cannot impartially inquire whether p. The first part of that is correct, but it denies his claim that no one believes p who does not act on it. The second is doubtful and irrelevant, too. It applies only if the examination is to be conducted by the owner personally.

Another point is made, but it is made in rebuttal of an imagined objection to his case, rather than as part of the positive argument for it. The objection is that there is nothing wrong with believing on insufficient evidence – as distinct from acting on the belief – because our beliefs are not public, but private matters of concern only to oneself. In rebuttal, Clifford claims that beliefs are not only private; for good or for ill, he says, our beliefs enter into the fabric of the heirloom which we acquire from, and transmit to, others. Clearly, that is true only of expressed and manifested beliefs, and, while it is plausible to say that no man's belief is in any case a purely private matter, it is not plausible to say that no belief of any man is a purely private matter.

Clifford disallows our third question, just as he did the second one. Belief on insufficient evidence, he responds, always has consequences for other people, always involves risk of harm to others. In support of that position, he makes the following case: first, that any instance of believing on insufficient evidence weakens one's powers of judiciously and fairly weighing evidence, or tends to make one credulous; second, that credulity in one person fosters a credulous character in others; and third, that credulity in one person encourages in others the dispositions to cheat and to lie. The last two claims are highly doubtful, the first one only a little less so. My credulity will not encourage credulity in others unless they know of it, and it may not even then. The same thing is true with the tendency to cheat and to lie. It is easy, moreover – returning to the first point – to overestimate the extent to which one instance of believing on insufficient evidence weakens one's practice of weighing evidence. I may be led so to regret the case that my resolve to inquire in other cases is strengthened rather than weakened by it.

One last point. It has been argued, against Clifford, that one can hold on insufficient evidence a belief which, because it is neither mentioned nor acted on, has no consequences for others. It is also quite possible to hold a belief, *action* upon which has no consequences for other people. I may, without checking my gesneriad handbook, believe that my ailing gloxinia requires watering and proceed to soak it thoroughly. My action may have devastating consequences for the plant, and important ones for me too, if it is my favourite. While it is easy to see that it may have consequences also for other people, it is not easy to see that it must do so. If it does not, then, although it may be said of me that I acted imprudently, it can scarcely be said that I acted immorally. The same would be true if, having consulted the handbook and read its warning against excessive watering, like Clifford's shipowner, I had nourished my belief by reflecting that the experts are not always right.

Clifford's argument for his position is, then, less than convincing. Moreover, the position itself is suspect. Suppose that his emigrants are worthy people fleeing from a cruel tyrant. Suppose that the oppressor is only hours away and that his aging vessel is their only means of possible escape from cruel torture and certain death. Surely it is not, then, obvious that the owner ought to take his vessel out of service and have her examined. If he cannot bring himself to let her sail with doubts about her condition still on his mind, surely it is not obvious that he would do wrong to nourish the belief that she will make it?

So much for Clifford's case. It is far from impeccable. James attacked it frequently, often with great vigour. Unfortunately, most of his blows sail very wide of the real target. We shall discuss them in a moment. Not all of his response is off the mark, however, and his failure to exploit some weaknesses in the opposition case is easily explained. The explanation is that he shares Clifford's view that no one believes p who is not ready to act on it. The best part of his response is his story of the Alpine Climber. Its point, as we have seen, is primarily prudential, not moral. A.C. would be foolish not to believe he can make the leap. It has a moral point too, however. In what A.C. did, James means, there was nothing morally wrong at all. Some other parts of James's attack are of considerable interest, despite being quite unsuccessful. They are of interest because they misrepresent Clifford so badly, because what they attack is so obviously a caricature. The interest is in the question how James could have done it. The explanation is again a simple one. This time it is that he read into Clifford the other part of his own view of belief, the part which Clifford did not hold.

One of these misrepresentations arises from simple exaggeration. Clifford condemned believing when the evidence is insufficient. That was his word. Later in the essay, he agreed that it was necessary to say what evidence *is* worthy, not enough just to say that it is wrong to believe on unworthy evidence.[4] He did try, even if he did not succeed. The point, however, is that nowhere does he even hint that believing is wrong when the evidence is less than conclusive, less than demonstrative. That is what James makes his opponents say, however. The following remark is a good example. "May it not be that in the theoretic life the man whose scruples about flawless accuracy of demonstration keep him forever shivering on the brink of Belief is as great an imbecile as the man at the opposite pole, who simply consults his prophetic soul for the answer to everything?"[5] With these sentiments Clifford could agree entirely. He does not insist on "flawless accuracy of demonstration." He requires that the evidence be sufficient, not that it be conclusive.

Frequently, James portrays his opponents as holding that the seeker after truth must turn himself into a passive recording machine. The following passage is a case in point. James introduces it by paraphrasing the position of the "anti-theistic wing" in language drawn from Huxley and from Clifford. That position is said to be that "it is base, it is vile, it is the lowest depth of immorality" to engage in wishful thinking; and we know already that there is a real difference between them on that topic. Then the description continues; "the mind must be a passive, reactionless sheet of white paper, on which reality will simply come and register its own philosophic definition, as the pen registers the curve on the sheet of a chronograph."[6] It is an easy position to refute. If the inquirer must be entirely passive, he must have no desires, must put no questions, must make no conjectures. Clearly, however, any inquirer must have some desire to find out, and he who puts no questions gets none answered; he who makes no conjectures gets none either confuted or confirmed. The wholly passive mind is not the ideal inquirer. The wholly passive mind is the non-inquirer. Clifford knows it as well as James does. One of his subtitles is "The Duty of Inquiry." The duty not to believe is not, for him, the duty to do nothing, to sit patiently waiting. It is the duty to go on inquiring, the duty, in other words, to make conjectures and to test hypotheses. James's portrayal of him is just a convenient whipping-boy, a figment of James's imagination, or better, as we shall see, of James's theory.

Another way of misrepresenting Clifford is to have him say that when the evidence is insufficient, we must suspend not just belief, but action also. James employs it often. The following passage is a good example: "suppose that, having just read 'The Ethics of Belief,' I feel it would be sinful to act upon an assumption unverified by previous experience – why, then ... I miss my foothold and roll into the abyss."[7] Now, no one should be led by a reading of Clifford to feel that it would be sinful to act on a proposition for which the evidence is insufficient to warrant belief. Clifford teaches no such thing. He insists that often it is "our duty to act upon probabilities, although the evidence is not such as to justify present belief; because it is precisely by such action, and by observation of its fruits, that evidence is got which may justify future belief."[8] Clifford is distinguishing between believing a proposition and acting on it, and making it clear that his thesis is about the former only, not the latter. Consistently with his insistence on a duty to inquire, he is saying that there is a duty to act on p when acting on it is a way of getting evidence about it. There is no "preposterous command that I shall stir neither hand nor foot, but remain balancing myself in eternal and insoluble doubt"[9]: and nothing, surely, could be wider of the mark than James's complaint that the "positivists ... condemn us to eternal ignorance for the 'evidence' which they wait for can never come so long as we are passive."[10] Clifford's thesis, to repeat the point, is that when the evidence is insufficient, we should refrain from believing and go on inquiring. It is not that we must do nothing but only wait, and it is not that we must refrain from acting when action is called for.

It is another distortion of Clifford's thesis to turn it into a prohibition against guessing or gambling. James does, and then rallies to their defence.[11] The concrete man, he says, has but one interest, to be right, and all means are fair which help him to it. One such means is "the rules of the scientific game." Another is guessing. If we are blessed with luck, guessing may be the thing to get us the truth, or to get it for us sooner. In that event, sticking to the rules of the scientific game will mean thinking more highly of the means than of the end it is designed to serve. So, James can say: "Were all of Clifford's works, except the 'Ethics of Belief,' forgotten, he might well figure in future treatises on psychology in place of the somewhat threadbare instance of the miser who has been led by the association of ideas to prefer his gold to all the goods he might buy therewith."[12]

More than one thing has gone wrong there, but the main point is again that Clifford is innocent of the charge. He does not condemn guessing and gambling any more than he condemns the other things which have been discussed. His paper is about the ethics of belief, and belief only. Why, then, does James read him as he does, read him so badly? The answer is that he reads into him his own view that no one acts on p who does not believe it. Give him that and it follows that the inquirer, the gambler, anyone who acts on p, also believes it. If the evidence does not favour p, he believes on insufficient evidence and what he does falls under Clifford's condemnation. It is a consequence, we saw James say earlier, of the fact that belief is measured by action, that he who forbids us to believe anything on insufficient evidence necessarily also forbids us to act as if it were true.[13] Clifford forbids the one but not the other. That is because he did not accept James's "fact." What James does is read it into him. That is what enables him to make Clifford forbid, not just belief, but action too. It is what enables him to paint him as the champion of passivity and patient waiting, the opponent of all conjecture and taking of chances.

By a nice irony, it is Clifford who gets the last laugh, however. Critics have read James's essay as a moral right-to-believe doctrine, as a reply to Clifford's moral duty-not-to-believe one. They have read it, in short, as a rival *ethics* of belief. It is that, in part, but in minor part. Taking Clifford as the foil distorts James's essay by highlighting the moral thesis and by putting the rest in shadow. To highlight what is central in it – the prudential thesis, the foolish-not-to-believe doctrine – the foil we need is Pascal.

CHAPTER TEN

Pascal

Pascal has not been used as the foil for James. That is a pity, for it is Pascal's pensée that best highlights features in his essay which hardly show up at all against the background of Huxley and Clifford.

There are several things about Pascal's argument that have to be noticed. One is that it develops through three stages.[1] Each stage draws the same conclusion, that it would be foolish not to gamble that God exists, that betting on God's existence is the wise bet. The first stage depends on the premise that, if we wager that God does exist, we lose nothing, even if He does not. That premise is deemed unacceptable to the sceptic and is dropped on that account. It is no part of the argument in its final form. The second stage depends on the premise that there is an even chance that God exists. That premise too, is deemed unacceptable to the sceptic and is dropped. It, too, is no part of the argument in its final form. The third and final stage consists of the claim that, even if there is something to lose, and even if the chance is minute that God exists, it is foolish not to gamble that He does, for if He does, the reward for so wagering is infinite in value. There are two claims that are crucial in that third stage. One is that there is some chance that God exists, however small. The other is that, if He does exist, the prize for betting that He does is infinite in value. The sceptic is assumed to grant both of them. He expresses no dissatisfaction with the argument in that form.

The second thing to notice about Pascal's argument is that it is about gambling, wagering, betting. That is generally accepted, but the corollary is not. The corollary is that it is not about believing. It is commonly portrayed as being about believing. That is how James portrays it. Translated freely, he says, Pascal's words are these; "You must either believe or not believe that God is – which will you do?"[2] That free translation is much too free. Translated still freely, but better, his words are, "You must wager either that God is or that He is not – which of these will you bet on?" Gambling is not believing. Ask the lucky punter how he knew his horse would win. "I didn't; it was pure gamble; I just took a chance on it," he replies. Ask him what made him think it would win, and his reply is the same. He did not know it and he did not think it either. It was pure gamble. That makes it clear that believing and gambling are not the same. It does more. It scotches the notion that it is by believing that we gamble. Our punter gambled. He did not believe. It was by putting his money on the line that he gambled. Gambling on God's existence is not by believing either. It, too, is by doing something, by putting something on the line.

The third thing to notice is seldom noticed, despite its obvious importance. In the argument, the prize is not a prize for believing. It is a prize for wagering, for gambling that God exists. The invitation which introduces the calculation goes like this: "Let us weigh gain and loss in calling heads that God is."[3] It is not the benefits of believing that are to be reckoned, but the benefits of "calling heads," of gambling. Appropriately, the advice which results from the calculation is, "Then do not hesitate, wager that He is";[4] or, "wherever there is infinity, and not an infinity of chances of loss against the chance of gain, there can be no hesitation, you must stake all."[5] The fact is that the word "believe" does not occur at all in the argument proper, in the exposition of the calculation. It occurs in the introduction, and it occurs in the sequel.

Finally, it should be noticed that the argument has a sequel. The argument proper is now complete; the sceptic expresses satisfaction with it, but he has, he says, a problem. He is so constituted that he cannot believe.[6] It is a curious response. What does he have to worry about if he cannot believe, but can wager? "Everything" would be the obvious answer, were the infinite reward tied to believing. It is not, however. As we have seen, it is tied to wagering. So, "nothing at all" is the correct answer. His problem is a non-problem – unless, of course, what he means is that he cannot bring himself to wager on God's existence. Pascal takes it that that is what he means, while still retaining the objector's word, "believe." That fact is nearly always missed, but it is clear enough in the text. The response to the problem is in two parts. The first is advice to get to understand his "inability to believe, since reason leads you to belief, and yet you cannot believe."[7] But it is not belief that reason has been shown to lead one to: it is wagering that God is. So, despite the word "believe," the advice is, and must be, to ponder his inability to gamble, since reason leads him to wager on God's existence, and yet he cannot do it. The second part of the response is no less significant. Wanting to have faith but incapable of it, he is advised to take a lesson from those who once were bound as he is but who now are cured of the disease of which he would be cured. The lesson is to follow the way by which they began. He is to do what believers do and that will bring him to belief. What deserves more, but gets less attention than that description of the remedy is the description of those he is to take as his models. "Take a lesson from those who have been bound like you, and who now stake all they possess."[8] The believers, those who have achieved faith, are those who *now* wager, who *still* wager. In Pascal's pensée, in short, wagering on God's existence is not the route that leads to something else, to faith. Wagering on God's existence is what faith is.

The passage is usually read quite differently. The sceptic is understood as saying that the only thing he cannot do is believe. He can wager. It is only believing that is a problem. The advice given him is understood as advice to wager on God's existence, as his models once did, and like them, in time, as a result, he will find himself believing. For reasons just given, that reading has to be rejected. His problem is not that he cannot believe, but can wager. It is that he cannot bring himself to wager on God's existence. So the reply is not at all that, if he will begin by wagering that God exists, he will find himself in time believing it. The reply is that, if he is nervous about wagering on God's existence, he will find it helps if he keeps in mind all those who have done it before him; and, if he fixes in mind those who are mature in faith, who now wager all they possess, it will help him to stake some small thing, to go take holy water and have masses said. The distinction to be drawn is not between wagering and believing. It is between wagering something on God's existence and wagering everything on it.

James devotes two paragraphs of his essay to Pascal. One is expository, the other critical. His exposition is loose and impressionistic, designed to convey only the gist of the original. That does not excuse the errors in detail which commentators have noted in it.[9] Rather than dwell on them, however, it is more useful to take note of three features of his account. One is his vacillation between "belief" and "wager." As we saw earlier, he expresses the option, wrongly, in terms of belief. The argument and the conclusion, however, he expresses, rightly, in terms of wagering, of staking something. The second is a related point. It is that he appears to follow the usual account of the sequel, to treat wagering as the prelude to faith, not as faith. The third is that the argument as he presents it corresponds essentially to the first stage of Pascal's argument, not the final one. It is true that the infinite gain is mentioned, true, also, that it is conceded that the chance that God exists may be minuscule, but what appears persistently is the premise of the first stage. "If you lose, you lose nothing at all," he says in presenting the argument. "At bottom, what have you to lose?" is the rhetorical question in which he sums it all up.[10]

The second paragraph is more difficult to interpret. There is no doubt that the impression which it conveys is one of rejection, of rejection on at least three different grounds. Not all of the negative comments, however, are attributed expressly to James himself. The first is introduced by the words, "You probably feel that ... " The second is introduced by "We feel that ... " The impression is undoubtedly given that James shares both feelings, and that they are entirely in order in both cases. No hint of a contrary indication is given anywhere in the passage. Accordingly, the paragraph is usually read as expressing James's own criticism as well as ours. "You probably feel," in short, is taken as "You will probably agree with my view that ... " Now, if that were the whole story, there would be no problem in interpreting the paragraph in that usual way. It is not the whole story, however. The other part of it is that James repeats in his own argument, and so endorses, the very features which, on that usual account of the paragraph, he finds fault with in Pascal's one.

To be clear about that, we need to look more closely at the passage.[11] The objections contained in it come to this:

1 It is to demean faith to make it speak in gambling language.
2 Faith "adopted wilfully after such a mechanical calculation" can be a sham only, a counterfeit faith.
3 Such calculation cannot issue in faith when there is no prior inclination to believe.

The thrust of (1) is not entirely clear. The objection may be to the *conception* of faith as gamble, or to an *apologetic* which advocates faith as the best bet, or to both. It is clear that if (2) is true as it stands, (3) goes without saying, for the calculation will not issue in genuine faith in any case. If (3) is meant to imply that the calculation *can* issue in faith when the hypothesis is live, (2) and (3) are incompatible and (2) needs amending by the addition of "except where there already exists some inclination to believe." Our task is to decide what, in these objections to Pascal, James can endorse without being the pot who calls the kettle black.

The following points are the relevant ones.

1 As we saw, earlier, James himself shows no hesitation whatsoever in sometimes making faith speak the language of the bettor at the race-track. The believer, he said, was backing the religious hypothesis against the field, the unbeliever the field against the religious hypothesis. Believer and unbeliever, alike, were gamblers, putting their money, as it were, on different horses.[12]

2 James described himself as long a defender of "the lawfulness of voluntarily adopted faith,"[13] so any objection he can have to a faith "adopted wilfully after such a mechanical calculation" can bear only on the later part of that phrase.

3 If "mechanical" is a reference to the mathematical character of the argument, it is not clear why being mechanical makes the calculation objectionable. If the objection is to the prudential character of the argument, James cannot endorse it, for his own argument is no less prudential. His case is that we are foolish if we do not believe. His reason is that we are better off if we do, that it is in our best interest to believe. That does not mean that James is just Pascal over again. There are differences, but, in both cases, the appeal is an appeal to self-interest. James is in no better position than Pascal to throw stones at Mrs Fairchild.[14]

4 What the last objection says about Pascal's argument, James says quite expressly about his own one. As he says, it also speaks "to the 'saving remnant' alone,"[15] to those for whom religion is a hypothesis that is in some measure live. So, if James can agree that what is said about Pascal is true, he can hardly agree that it is objectionable.

There is reason, then, to read James's paragraph on Pascal as an expression of plausible, and perhaps common, reactions to Pascal's argument rather than as a statement of his own response to it. The fact is that his own case is essentially similar to Pascal's, although not identical. One difference is this. In Pascal the emphasis is on the post-mortem benefits of wagering that God is. It is not solely upon these. It is Pascal, after all, who asks "What harm will you get in following this line?" and who, claiming that you will be faithful, honest, humble, grateful, beneficent, a good friend, true, and with pleasures of all kinds except the poisonous ones, answers "I tell you that you will gain in *this* life."[16] In Pascal's presentation, however, that is not the main point. In James's it is. His case is that we are better off even now,[17] better off betting on God's existence than not doing so, and better off even if later we are proved wrong. The crux of James's case, but not of Pascal's, is that if we lose we lose nothing, that in betting on God's existence, even if we lose, we gain.

Here it is worth taking up a point which we omitted earlier from James's statement of his case that faith and working hypothesis are one and the same thing. There, after making faith say that it expects the future to vindicate it, he makes it add the following: "but if it should turn out, as indeed it may, that I have spent my days in a fool's paradise, why, better have been the dupe of *such* a dreamland than the cunning reader of a world like that which then beyond all doubt unmasks itself to view."[18] It is clearly an important part of James's account of faith. It was omitted earlier only because it weakens rather than strengthens the case he was then presenting. No scientist says he is better off with the wrong hypothesis than with the right one. The reason for mentioning it at this point is its close fit with James's present claim that we are better off betting on God's existence, even if we lose the bet. The fit is not perfect. It is the language of belief that is used, not that of the gaming table. Otherwise, however, the claim is the same.

There are reasons why Pascal has not been used as the foil for James. One is that Clifford has been given the rôle. When that is done, James's essay is read as an *ethics* of belief, not as prudence, not as economics. Not only so, it is read as an ethics of *belief*. Clifford was dealing with belief and belief only, so James was dealing with that, too. Read against the background of Huxley and Clifford, neither the prudentialism of James's position nor its gaming-table talk stand out as the important features that they are. Since they are the features which connect it with Pascal, that connection is underplayed, too. The other reason why Pascal is not used to illumine James is that James himself discourages it. In his paragraph on Pascal, he appears anxious to disown any family connection, not to claim it. The effect is to discourage looking for resemblances. If one is not discouraged, one finds resemblances aplenty. It is a presupposition of Pascal's argument that reason cannot settle the question whether God exists or not. The same is true of James's argument. His "cannot by its nature be decided on intellectual grounds" is twin to Pascal's "Reason can settle nothing here."[19] There *is* something that reason can do, however. It can, Pascal says, tell us what to *do*. It tells us to wager that God is. James's essay says the same thing. It says we are foolish if we do not believe. It is true that the verbs there are different – "wager" in Pascal, "believe" in James – but they are not different at all if we take seriously James's description of the believer as the gambler. Even if one looks no further than James's thesis statement, one finds reminders of Pascal. "Forced," in James, connects with Pascal's "Yes, but wager you must";[20] "live" and "living" match his requirement that *some* chance must be assigned to God's existence and "momentous" is a reflection, if a pale one, of Pascal's talk of infinite gain.

It is not the similarities in detail that are to be stressed, however, but the broad family resemblance, the prudentialism of both arguments and their willingness to treat faith as gamble. These are the things in James's essay that get lost in the shadows when Clifford is made the foil. They show up brightly in the light cast by Pascal.[21]

CHAPTER ELEVEN

Bain

Throughout the second half of the nineteenth century, Alexander Bain promoted an account of belief which was novel and influential. The subject was a contentious one. As Bain saw it, he was opposing a majority view which treated belief as a function of the intellect. His own view was that it was a function of the will. His treatment of belief, accordingly, comes not in that volume of his psychology called *The Senses and the Intellect*, but in the other half of it called *The Emotions and the Will*. The chapter on belief underwent revision as the book was reissued in new editions. The discussion which follows is based not on any one of them but, mainly, on the chapter in the 1872 edition of his *Mental and Moral Science*. That is the edition of that work to which Bain added an appendix which began with the words, "In the chapter on Belief, I have given what I now regard as a mistaken view of the fundamental nature of the state of Belief ..."[1] That appendix has been regarded as his "recantation."[2] It is less than clear that it really is that. Even if it is a recantation, it still makes sense to choose a pre-recantation text, for it is the pre-recantation Bain who is the interesting one. *Mental and Moral Science* was designed as a condensation and as a teaching aid. It is arranged as numbered sentences followed by exposition which provides the interpretation or the argument. I shall refer to these as "text" and "commentary." It is the first two texts together with their commentaries which are of major interest. They contain two important doctrines. One is a claim about the definition of belief. The other is a claim about the test of belief. They are interwoven in Bain's presentation, but easily separated. Let us begin with the discussion of definition.

There is a story commonly told about Bain, and it goes like this. He had an original definition of belief. To believe p, his view was, means to act on p when the occasion arises. He said as much when he said in his second text that "*what we believe we act upon*,"[3] and he did the same when he said, in the commentary, that the differentia of belief is "acting, or being prepared to act, when the occasion arises."[4] His definition was not only an original one, the story proceeds, it was also of an original kind. It treated belief as a disposition when it was common to regard it as an activity, and, in that respect, it is a pioneering one. Bain did not simply assert his definition, the story ends, he argued for it. In particular, he showed himself aware of some, at least, of the difficulties in his view and defended his definition against several objections to it.[5] It is by no means – on the face of it – an unflattering story, but things look differently when we look a bit closer.

What, let us ask, were the objections which Bain anticipated to his definition and how did he respond to them? One of them goes like this. Surely, it cannot be true that believing p means acting on p when the occasion arises, if it is true, as it is, that people do believe p but fail to act on it when the occasion arises? Another goes like this. Surely, it cannot be true that believing p means acting on p when the occasion arises, if it is true, as again it is, that all of us do believe things which we cannot possibly act on because the occasion for our acting on them cannot possibly arise. Both of them look like good objections. Bain's view is said to be that they are "apparent exceptions" to his definition, but not real ones. The interest is in how he argues the case. Bain's replies – although, for obvious reasons, they are not usually so stated – come to the following. The fact that we believe things which we fail to act on when the occasion has arisen, is not inconsistent with the claim that believing p means acting on it when the occasion arises, for it is entirely consistent with the different claim that believing p means having some inclination (but not an omnipotent one) to act on it when the occasion arises. As he says, "We are inclined to act where we believe, but not always with an omnipotent strength of impulse."[6] Bain's second reply comes to this. The fact that we believe things "that we never can have any occasion to act upon" is not inconsistent with the definition of belief as acting on p when the occasion arises, for it is entirely consistent with the different claim that "X believes p" means "X would act on p if the occasion were to arise." As he says, "We express the attitude by saying, that *if* we went to Africa, we would do certain things in consequence of the affirmation."[7]

The flattering story has now acquired touches of the grotesque. That is not because the replies cited are not the replies Bain makes. They *are* the replies he makes. What causes the trouble is a mistaken assumption. It is that Bain is defending a definition of belief against objections to it. He is not. What he is defending is a statement *about* the definition of belief, not a statement *of* it. He is defending the claim that no definition of belief can be a satisfactory one which does not include some reference to action. Recognize that fact, and his discussions, not only of the two "apparent exceptions" already mentioned, but of the other two as well, begin to look a lot better than they did.

The first two come to this. There are reasons for thinking that belief can be defined without mentioning action. One reason is that we can believe things which we do not act on when the occasion arises. Another is that we can believe things that we can never have any occasion to act on. These reasons are not good reasons, however, although the facts are quite correct. They are not good reasons because, in the first case, we believe only if we have some inclination to act on it, and, in the second, we believe only if we should act on it were the occasion to arise. So both cases confirm, as Bain would put it, that belief, in its essential import, is related somehow to activity. Incidentally, Bain's discussion of his second case makes it pretty clear where his interest lies. "It is not hard," he says, "to trace a reference to action in every one of these beliefs."[8] That is what he does – trace *some* reference to action – and, given his purpose, that is all he needs to do.

Suppose he is defending a statement about the definition of belief. Is he not also defending a definition of it, the view that believing p means acting on it when the occasion arises? Hardly. He has conceded perfectly valid "real exceptions" to that definition, and it is the oddest way of defending any definition to replace it by a different one and then by a different one still. One does not defend the claim that believing p means acting on it when the occasion arises by saying either that it means that one has some inclination to act on it, or that one would act on it if the occasion were to arise.

Bain's two other apparent exceptions are sufficiently similar to let us treat them together also. One is the claim that belief is simply a feeling or feelings, that emotion alone will constitute belief. The argument quoted in support is that belief must be a feeling because our beliefs often are influenced by our feelings. Bain responds neatly: "The fact is admitted, but not the inference."[9] He then promises to show later how our feelings can influence our beliefs "without themselves constituting the state of believing."[10] His other apparent exception is the claim that belief is simply an intellectual power, that the intellect alone will constitute belief. The main argument quoted is that belief must be simply an intellectual power, because it is often by a purely intellectual process that we come to believe. In geometry, we come to believe q as a result of coming to see that it follows from p. Bain rejects the argument, replying that if we come to believe q as a result of seeing that it follows from p, we do so only because we already believe p. "The reasonings of the Geometer do not create the state of belief," he says, "they merely bring affirmations under an already-formed belief, the belief in the axioms of the science."[11] He shows himself aware that that does not close the subject, and again promises to show later the precise function of our intelligence in believing. If we ask the question, to what are these views – that belief is purely emotional, that it is purely intellectual – apparent exceptions, the answer is obvious. They are apparent exceptions to the claim that belief is partly behavioural, a matter of activity. If they are true, moreover, they are real exceptions to it, not just apparent ones. What Bain does is deny that they are true. That is what he is bound to do if he wants to defend his claim about the definition, his claim that belief, in its essential import, is related to activity.

There is a second quite different doctrine about belief in Bain's passage. It is that action is the test of belief. In Bain the doctrine covers two things. One is that we do not really believe p if we are not ready to act on it. The other is that we do believe p if we are ready to act on it. Take his case of the general who says his position is stronger than the enemy's, but who acts as if it were weaker.[12] We say, Bain claims – and he means we are right to say it – that he does not believe it is stronger, and that he does believe it is weaker. The action test, in short, is not just a negative test, but a positive one, too. It is our way of telling that people do not believe things they say they believe. It is also our way of telling that people do believe things they deny believing.

The doctrine is mistaken in both of its parts. If someone does not act on something which he asserts, or says he believes, we do not *always* say that he does not believe it. Sometimes we say, "I just don't know what he believes, what to make of him." We say that, not because we have no indicators, but because the indicators we have point in opposite directions. Sometimes we say that he really does believe it, despite his actions. We often do that if we can find some explanation for his behaviour. "He really does believe in free trade; he voted against that free-trade measure because he thought it too weak or inopportune or ..." Sometimes we say it, even when we can find no explanation. "He really does believe in free trade, so he must have had his reasons, although I cannot think what they could have been." Some, no doubt, will sometimes think us naive for saying that sort of thing. The fact remains, however, that we do say it, often rightly, and that Bain is just wrong when he denies it. The other part of the claim is mistaken too. If someone who denies believing p acts on it, we do not always say that he believes it. Remember the gambler and the scientific inquirer. If the gambler says it was pure gamble, that he did not believe his horse would win when he put his money on it, we believe him. We do the same with the scientist. If he says he just had a hunch, that he did not believe his hypothesis when he set about testing the wallpaper for arsenic, we believe him too.

There is one more element in Bain's account of belief which deserves mention. It is his doctrine of primitive credulity.[13] Its essential claim is that we do not *acquire* belief, we start with it. What we acquire is doubt. To think of something is also to believe it; moreover, it is to go on believing it until something happens to make us doubt it. Bain is rejecting the view that we begin by wondering whether something is true, and grow gradually into belief as the evidence for it accumulates. We begin, his view is, by believing it and get drawn into doubt by the checks which experience provides. He refers to it as "this method of believing first and proving afterwards."[14] The reversal means that the rôle of experience is seen very differently. What experience does is disabuse us of false beliefs, not engender in us true ones. "Sound belief," he writes, "instead of being a pacific and gentle growth, is in reality, the battering of a series of strongholds, the conquering of a country in hostile occupation."[15]

Finally on Bain, some brief observations on the question of the "recantation."

1 It has been held that what he recanted was his claim about the definition of belief. After 1872, it is said, that claim disappears from his discussions of the subject.[16] It does not disappear. The new Bain insists as firmly as the old one had that "readiness to act is thus what makes belief something more than fancy," that "we must not depart from their reference to action ... otherwise they lose their fundamental character as things credited, and pass into mere fancies, and the sport of thinking."[17] Whatever Bain recanted, that is not it.

2 It was "one of the very nicest of problems," Bain remarked, "to say in which of the departments of the mind – Feeling, Action, Intellect – Belief has its immediate origin."[18] On that question, the statements of the old Bain and of the new one *are* strikingly different. Pre-1872, the claim is that belief is a "phase of our active nature."[19] Post-1872, it is that it is "a fact or incident of our intellectual nature."[20]

3 What is not clear is that Bain's views before and after 1872 are correspondingly different, or indeed, any different. The question asked by the old Bain is whether belief is a state purely intellectual or intellectual and something besides.[21] His answer is that it is intellectual and something besides. The new Bain does not hold belief to be purely intellectual any more than the old one had held it to be purely non-intellectual. His view continues to be that belief is intellectual and something besides.

4 It is the adversary who has changed. The old Bain was combatting the view of metaphysicians generally who had been "almost, if not altogether, unanimous in enrolling belief among the intellectual powers."[22] A forthright, if incautious, way of underlining his opposition to that view is to call it "a phase of our active nature." The new Bain is combatting the view that "Belief is purely an incident of our activity."[23] A forthright, but equally incautious, way of underlining one's opposition to *that* view is to call it "an incident of our intellectual nature." In short, Bain's statements can change while his official view remains the same.

5 There is something more, however. Bain accepted as "the view promulgated by me," the view "that Belief is *purely* an incident of our activity."[24] He could have cried "Foul" and cited much evidence in support. Instead, he accepts the description without a whisper of protest. The reason, quite clearly, is that the new Bain had been made to see that the old one had also said things which implied that belief is purely non-intellectual.

James, we know, studied Bain, lectured on him, and set his students examination questions on the differences between his own account of belief and Bain's account. So, what is different between them, and what is similar?

James did not share Bain's view about the definition of belief. He sided, rather, with Bain's opponents, with Mill and Sully, whose view was that belief is simple, unanalysable, indefinable.[25] Given that view, it had to be a mistake to hold, as Bain had, that a reference to action is part of the meaning of belief, no matter what form the reference might take. If belief was indefinable, believing p could not mean "acting on it when the occasion arises," or "having some inclination to act on it when the occasion arises," or "would act on it if the occasion were to arise," or "would have some inclination to act on it if the occasion were to arise." If it was indefinable, no definition would do.

James was in total agreement with Bain that action is the test of belief. If we are not ready to act on something, we do not believe it; if we are ready to act on it, we do believe it. It is that second part that is the crucial one. It is what leads James to call any one who is ready to act on something a "believer" – including the gambler and the scientific inquirer – despite the protestations they might make to the contrary. Explaining why James called "believers" people who are not believers, it explains, also, why one must ask whether his essay is really about belief.

He also endorsed Bain's doctrine of primitive credulity.[26] The surprising thing is that he did not use it as he might have done. If credulity is primitive, the fact is that sometimes we cannot help believing on insufficient evidence. In that case, it cannot always be morally wrong to do it.[27]

CHAPTER TWELVE

Renouvier and Pragmatism

Writing to Peirce about Renouvier, James said of his will-to-believe essay, "The whole of my essay ... is cribbed from him."[1] Writing to Renouvier, he said much the same thing rather more formally. "I sent you a *New World* the other day, however, with an article in it called 'The Will to Believe' in which (if you took the trouble to glance at it) you probably recognized how completely I am still your disciple."[2] It is surprising how little these remarks have been pondered, weighed, and sifted. When they have been noted, their importance has been discounted. In part, that is due to James's reputation for confessing to more obligations than he owed.[3] Mainly it is for another reason. The essay is assumed to be pragmatism applied to religion,[4] if not Peirce's pragmatism, then James's one. If it is that, it is a home brew, not a foreign import. What follows is, first, a number of observations about pragmatism. They are meant to endorse James's advice that pragmatism and the will-to-believe doctrine are better kept apart. They are also meant to say about pragmatism as much as is needed to show that no more needs to be said about it. After that, there is something more about James's remarks on Renouvier.

Some of James's contemporaries thought that his pragmatism just was his will-to-believe doctrine, and said so. One of them said so in a paper[5] which James dismissed as a "really farcical interpretation."[6] For that critic, the main thesis of pragmatism was to be found, as he said, "stated with all Professor James's peculiar vigour and humour, in the opening essay of his volume, *The Will to Believe*"; and that main thesis of pragmatism consisted in the claim, as he phrased it, that "our emotional nature has a right to decide for us to what beliefs we shall commit ourselves."[7] One commentator who thought mistaken those who thus identified pragmatism and the will-to-believe doctrine, wrote to James asking him to adjudicate. James replied that the two doctrines were very different and better kept apart. The will-to-believe doctrine, he explained, had to do with "the policy of belief." Pragmatism had to do with something else, with the "constitution of truth." They were not at all the same thing, and the will-to-believe matter should not be permitted, in his words, to "complicate the question of what we mean by truth."[8]

There is a common practice which completely subverts that reply from James. It is to give an account of James's pragmatism using his will-to-believe essay as a source. The two doctrines as a result become indistinguishable. The practice is justified if the essay *is* an expression of pragmatism, if it is, as it has been called, James's "first *application* of Peirce's pragmatism and one which he never entirely succeeded in discarding."[9] It is justified only if something of that sort is true. Often, the question is not even asked, just begged. That is surprising, given James's warning to keep the two doctrines apart. What is not surprising is that when the practice is followed, pragmatism becomes, in the phrase of one of them, the view that "some *un*reasoned beliefs are, in some sense or other, justifiable."[10] That will do tolerably well for the essay. It will not do at all for pragmatism.

Seldom defended, the practice is, moreover, indefensible. That is not just because James says that it is. There is another reason. There are texts in which James expounds pragmatism and illustrates it by reference to religion. One of these is his 1898 lecture, "Philosophical Conceptions and Practical Results," designed to introduce Peirce and pragmatism to the Californians.[11] The other is the chapter "Pragmatism and Religion" in his *Pragmatism* book. What is striking is how very different these are from the will-to-believe essay. In the California address, what James argues is that theism and materialism mean different things and how it can be shown that they do. It is an exercise, in Peirce's words, in how to make these ideas clear. It argues neither that we ought to, nor that we may, believe either theism or materialism. The same is true of the book chapter. Earlier in the book James has argued that, for pragmatism, "true" means "works." He now says that, if religion works, it is true. Consistency requires him to assert that hypothetical. He does not go beyond it. He does say of the religious hypothesis that "experience shows that it certainly does work."[12] He does not conclude that it is, therefore, true, or that we should think it true. Instead, he refers immediately to the *problem* of so formulating theism that it "will combine satisfactorily with all the other working truths."[13] What works, in short, may not work "satisfactorily in the widest sense of the word,"[14] and no claim short of the latter is tantamount to a claim of truth.

In James, pragmatism is a theory of meaning which became, in particular, a theory of the meaning of truth. In capsule, the theory is that "true" means "works." Russell considered that it was the product of not one confusion but a multitude of them, and, although many have tried, not many critics of James have succeeded in adding significantly to his list. A constant refrain is that it depends on confusing "meaning" and "criterion" or "test." To check whether a library has a certain book, Russell explained, we look it up in the card catalogue, but it is, nevertheless, a mistake to think that "is listed in the card catalogue" means the same thing as "is in the library."[15] To check a hypothesis, we inquire whether it works theoretically – whether all of its verifiable consequences are true and none false – but it is, nevertheless, a mistake to think that "true" means the same thing as "works theoretically." It further compounds the mistake, he added, to confuse theoretical working with practical working and think that "true" means "satisfying our emotional needs" or "facilitating a virtuous life."[16]

To the central part of that critique, one respondent attempted a brave defence. It is a mistake – a "howler" he called it – to say that "true" means "works" or "is useful," but it is a mistake, he insisted, of which James was innocent. He was as innocent of it as Mill was of a similar one. Mill had been criticized for holding that "right" means "useful," when he had, in fact, said nothing of the sort. What he had said is that being useful is the criterion, the test of rightness. In the same way, James had been criticized for holding that "true" means "works," when he also had been holding only that working or utility is the criterion of truth.[17] Admittedly, the crime was a crime, but the client had not committed it.

The trouble with that defence is that the client had already admitted everything, and had given not the slightest sign of repentance. Replying to Russell, James had said that the pragmatist claim was that "true" means "working," not anything less than that, and he had made himself pretty clear on the point. Working, he said, was not proposed "merely as a sure sign, mark, or criterion, by which truth's presence is habitually ascertained"[18] as listing in the card catalogue is a sign, mark, or criterion by which a book's presence in a library is habitually ascertained. It was proposed as the *causa existendi*,[19] not merely as the *causa cognoscendi* of true beliefs. "True," in short, *means* "works," and it does so even if most people are unaware that in saying that something is true they are saying that it works, and even if people call things true without first checking to see if they work.

James thought that Peirce's pragmatic maxim had given expression to a practice which the English-speaking philosophers had followed by instinct.[20] It is instructive to review what he saw as examples of their prevenient pragmatism. One example is Locke on personal identity. A second is Berkeley on matter. Another is Hume on causation, and Bain also gets a mention, doubtless for his account of belief. In James's expositions, there is a common pattern. Memory is not just the sign of personal identity, that identity consisting in something else, the oneness of a mental substance. Memory is what constitutes personal identity. Our sensible impressions are not just the sign of the presence of a physical object, the object being something other than the collection of impressions. A congeries of sensible impressions is what a material object is. Regular succession is not just the sign of a causal connection between events, that connection being something other than regular succession. Regular succession is what causation is. What is common to all these cases is this; what had been regarded not as the meaning but as a criterion only is now taken as the meaning. The implication for "truth" of these "preluders" of pragmatism is clear enough. It is that working is not just the criterion of truth, but the meaning of truth. "Now if pragmatists only affirmed that utility is a *criterion* of truth," Russell had written, "there would be much less to be said against their view."[21] Perhaps that really is right, but as James saw it, those same words had been sounded before and philosophy had made progress by disregarding them.[22]

If "true" means "works," the next question is what "works" means. James had a three letter word for what critics had said about this. The word was "rot." He was right. It was rot, and – too bad for him – very persistent rot. Russell exemplified it in his charge that pragmatism confused theoretical with practical working and so held that something is true if believing it makes for an emotionally or morally better life. It was witless caricature which, James said, cast "a lurid light" on the ability of philosophers to understand one another.[23] Certainly, it was not what he had said. What he had said was that a *scientific hypothesis* properly will not be accounted true unless it meets two conditions. It must be consistent with our existing body of truths or disturb it as little as possible. It must also be consistent with new fact. These two requirements meant, he thought, that our scientific theories are wedged in as little else is. Sometimes, however, more than one hypothesis will meet the conditions and, *then*, we choose between them on grounds of taste, preferring the simpler, the more elegant of the two.[24] What he was not saying is that a scientific hypothesis is properly accounted true if it is simple and elegant, even if it is inconsistent with our other truths and with experience. About *metaphysical* theories he said something a little different. When two of these fit equally well with our existing body of truths, logical and scientific, and with new fact, that one of them will properly be accounted true which better satisfies our emotional and moral requirements. What he was not saying is that in metaphysics anything is properly accounted true if we find it emotionally and morally useful to believe it, no matter how inconsistent it may be with all our other truths and experiences. "My position," he wrote, "is that *other things equal*, emotional satisfactions count for truth ... "[25] Or again, more fully and pointedly, "When I *say* that, *other things being equal*, the view of things that seems more satisfactory morally will legitimately be treated by men as truer than the view that seems less so, *they quote me as saying* that anything morally satisfactory can be treated as true, no matter how unsatisfactory it may be from the point of view of its consistency with what we already know or believe to be true about physical or natural facts. Which is rot!!"[26]

Our theme has been that pragmatism is one thing, the will-to-believe doctrine another. That was James's view and Perry knew it. He was not quite persuaded, however. The letter to Kallen, he agreed, divides the doctrines, but it also points the way, he added, to their union.[27] It is not clear that the doctrines need to be united, or that they can be. There is no inconsistency, real or apparent, between them, no need, therefore, to argue that they are consistent. On the other hand, little promise attaches to any plan to show them to be one and the same. The one argues that we ought to believe theism when as yet we have no intellectual ground for believing it. The other defines "true" as "works" and says a good deal about the grounds for calling things true. Perry's explanation is that what will unite them is "the generalized idea of truth as the goodness of ideas on the whole, where agreement with fact, though it may take precedence, is only one value among others."[28] The one doctrine will encompass the other one. If that is Perry's suggestion, two things are wrong. As the definition of truth is generalized, more and more things become intellectual grounds for believing a proposition, including those things which, according to the other doctrine, justify belief in the absence of intellectual grounds. Expand far enough the grounds for calling something true, and the will-to-believe doctrine is squeezed out by the other one, not encompassed within it. The other thing is that the account given of pragmatism is still too close to the one James called "rot." For him, no proposition is to be called true if it lacks agreement with fact. That is a sine qua non. None of the other values is that. They get into the game at all only as tie-breakers when two hypotheses are equal in that other, essential respect.

Now it is time to return to James's confession of larceny. There is an argument in Renouvier with which he was familiar as early as 1870, and which impressed him very deeply.[29] It is an argument for belief in freedom. What James did in his will-to-believe essay is adapt it to his own purpose and make of it an argument for belief in God.

The argument goes like this. The choice between freedom and determinism is one which we cannot avoid making. The alternatives are mutually exclusive and collectively exhaustive. So, if we choose, we must choose the one or the other. We cannot, moreover, afford not to choose. On some questions we can suspend judgment, and often that is the right course. On other questions, however, including this one, suspending judgment is a fatal course. Here are Renouvier's words.

La liberté et la nécessité ne sauraient être ni simultanément vraies, ni simultanément fausses, car, de deux choses l'une, ou les actes humains sont *tous et totalement* prédéterminés par leurs conditions et antécédents, ou ils ne le sont pas *tous et totalement.* C'est ainsi que se pose la question logique. Le doute serait donc notre seule ressource: mais le doute ne nous tire point de peine quant à la morale: s'il est souvent légitime en face des théories, il est la mort de l'âme dans les choses pratiques et touchant toute croyance d'où dépend la conduite de la vie.[30]

In James's language, that is the claim that the choice between freedom and determinism is a forced option.

Can the decision be made on intellectual grounds? Renouvier's answer is that it cannot. There is, he holds, no way of demonstrating the one position or the other one. "Impossibilité de démontrer la liberté," he writes, "aussi bien que de démontrer la nécessité."[31] An appeal to experience serves no better. "La liberté ne se démontre pas; elle ne se constate pas davantage à la manière d'un fait."[32] The choice between freedom and determinism, then, is not only a forced option. It is, in Renouvier, a forced option which cannot be decided on intellectual grounds.

How, then, is the matter to be decided, since it must be decided? By affirming freedom, Renouvier replies, and because the belief in freedom brings benefits not afforded by believing determinism. This is how he puts it:

Dans l'impuissance de rien démontrer, l'unique ressource qui reste est d'affirmer la liberté à titre de postulat. La vérité, non pas prouvée, mais réclamée et digne d'être choisie, est celle qui pose un fondement pour la morale et aussi un fondement pour la connaissance pratique, indépendament de laquelle on ne peut asseoir "la science".[33]

That, clearly, is the claim that, since the option is forced and cannot be decided on intellectual grounds, the wise choice is to believe the alternative which it benefits us the more to believe.

That account is not a complete account of Renouvier's argument for belief in freedom. It does not pretend to be. It is a major part of that argument, however. Its resemblance to James's argument in his will-to-believe essay is clear enough to leave no ground for doubting the correctness of James's assertion that his argument was "cribbed" from Renouvier. In this case, at least, the obligation he confessed was certainly owed.

CHAPTER THIRTEEN

Two Critics

James's essay has never been lacking in critics. Soon after its publication, he was, he said, "in much hot water" over it,[1] and, ever since, that has continued to be true. Much comment on it, in his day and in ours also, is useful only if one has a malevolent interest in showing how far philosophical misunderstanding can go.[2] Some of it is highly instructive, however. Two of the more valuable critics are Dickinson Miller and C.J. Ducasse. Miller published two papers on James's essay some forty years apart. The first one, published in 1899, James dismissed rather too lightly. The second, published in 1942, was and remains one of the best critical accounts of the essay. Miller sent a copy of it to Ducasse who expressed his almost total agreement with it.[3] There was one point in the essay, however, which he thought a sound one, and he said so. Some ten years later, Ducasse sent Miller the typescript of his book, *A Philosophical Scrutiny of Religion*, and invited him to write a foreword to it. Miller, acknowledging the invitation as "the highest philosophical honour I have ever received," replied that he was "flatly and insuperably debarred from doing what I want to do."[4] The reason was that, admirable as he found the book to be in other respects, it showed tendencies which ran counter to some of his own most deeply held convictions. One of these was Ducasse's readiness to find something sound in James's will-to-believe doctrine. The correspondence continued in an exchange of letters in which Ducasse kept pushing and Miller kept resisting the claim that there is one sound point. "I hold that *none* of James's arguments are sound," Miller insisted in one of the letters.[5] He was not willing to give an inch. An inch, Ducasse suggested, was all he was asking him to give, to concede *one* sound point amid all the "confusions and errors in James's essay,"[6] and that point one which had "nothing to do with volition to believe or with a right to will to believe."[7] Put that way, it sounded little enough, but Miller remained unmoved. What follows is not a running commentary either on Miller's papers or on the Miller-Ducasse correspondence. Its interest in them is a quite selective one. Its business is with those parts only which bear on the question what the essay is about if it is not about belief.

Ducasse's first letter is the one which set out most fully the "one important and sound point" which he found in James's essay. It will occupy us in a moment. It is worth noting first, however, a curious contradiction between his opening and his closing references to it. In introducing the point, he describes it as having "nothing to do with volition to believe or with a right to will to believe." That is the description of it which suggests that in asking Miller to concede it, he was asking him to concede very little. In closing his letter, however, he describes it as "the sound idea ... which vindicates something that might be not inaptly described as ... a right to believe."[8] On that account, surely, it was not just an inch he was asking Miller to give, but a mile.

The one sound point, he said, is that "there are cases in human affairs where decision has to be pure gamble."[9] He defined the cases and gave the following example. You are on a street car going down hill when the brakes suddenly fail. Only two courses are open to you, to jump off or to stay on. If you cannot decide which of those to do, you will end up doing exactly what you would have done if you had made the decision to stay on. Not being a student of traffic accident statistics, you have no ground at all – nor can you quickly enough get any – for believing that either course is safer than the other. In cases like that one, whatever decision you make, you gamble.

So far, there is nothing at all about believing, beyond the claim that if you believe either, your belief is groundless. That is as it should be. When your decision is pure gamble, you do not believe that either course is the safer one. You take a chance on its being the safer one, and that you do not by believing something which you have no ground for believing. You do it by jumping or by deciding to stay with the car. So, if the one sound point is that there are cases where decision has to be pure gamble, there is nothing in it about belief, and Ducasse is right in saying that the point has nothing to do with volition to believe or with a right to will to believe.

Let us see how the statement continues. It continues with the claim that "although pure gamble is, by definition, non-rational in the sense that the alternative one chooses to bet on is not known to be more probably true than the other; yet pure gamble may be rational in another sense."[10] It will be rational in this second sense, Ducasse explains, if, "irrespective of whether one loses or wins one's bet, some immediate reward is known to be attached to *the act itself of betting* on a given side, whereas no such reward, or a lesser one, is attached to the act of betting on the other side."[11] That claim can be made more concrete by adding one new feature to Ducasse's example. Suppose I have reason to believe that a lawsuit against the streetcar company is likely to be successful if my injuries are sustained while I am on board their property, and less likely to succeed if they result from my jumping off or from my being hit by passing traffic. An immediate reward now attaches to betting one way and it makes staying on board the rational bet to make. It does nothing, however, to make it rational for me to believe, or try to believe, that I am safer on the streetcar than off it. So there is still nothing about volition to believe or about the right to will to believe. The claim, moreover, is an "ought" claim, not just a "right" one, and what I ought to do is bet a certain way, not believe or try to believe a certain proposition.

For the sake of argument, let us assume that the religious option fits Ducasse's description and that a decision about it, therefore, has to be pure gamble. Let us assume, also, that some immediate reward attaches to betting on God's existence, none to betting against it. What follows is that it will be rational to bet that God exists and irrational to bet against it. Nothing follows about believing that God exists, about willing to believe it, or about a right to will to believe it. How, then, does Ducasse make the move from betting to believing? He gives a new example. If a person has some belief in God, he says, and that belief has the effect of making him happier, more courageous, more beneficent than he would otherwise be, it will be rational for him to do what he can to cultivate that belief despite its being unsupported by any balance of evidence. What has happened there to smooth the move from betting to believing is that the immediate reward which, in his description and in his original example, attached to betting one way, has become, in this example, attached to believing one proposition. The result is that for the first time, we do have something about believing.

The move depends on two assumptions, both of them false. One is that we cannot act on a proposition without believing it. The other is that an immediate reward attaches not to betting that God exists, but only to believing that He does. Miller rejected the first one. In response to Ducasse's suggestion that non-belief means non-action – "the inaction which such suspense [of judgment] motivates" – Miller rightly says that we "may *try* [an action] because attractive, not on any probability – and without belief."[12] The second assumption is also false. In Ducasse's first example as we modified it, it is by staying on board, not by believing that we are safer there, that we improve our chance of successful litigation against the transportation company. No doubt, some benefits attach to believing that God exists which do not attach to betting that He does. That is not true, however, of the one which plays a rôle in James's argument. To retain whatever chance there is of making the gods' acquaintance, what we need is not, as James wrongly says, to believe that

God exists, but only to act on it, and that we do if we bet on His existence. In sum, what Ducasse's sound point vindicates is something about betting that God exists, not something about believing it.

In his first paper, Miller complained that it is not easy to be sure what James's doctrine really is. The basic problem is "whether the author means that we are to bring ourselves by use of will into a believing state of mind, an internal assent, or only that we are to act as if we believed."[13] He noted that a critic in the *Nation* had taken the second view, and conceded that "much vigorous writing could be cited to either effect."[14] He himself decided for the first one; "it would seem that it is no mere outward scheme of living, without an *ex animo* assent, that is recommended, but action flowing from and expressing a state of mind which is none the less belief because it rises superior to the evidence."[15] On that view, the doctrine is about resolving to believe, "to kill a doubt we have and breed a belief we as yet have not."[16] On the other, it is about resolving "not to believe, but to act as if certain propositions were true ... though we freely and mentally admit the while that they are entirely doubtful."[17] Miller defends his preference by citing some frequently recurring expressions which contain the word "believe." Also in support, he cites what is surely the double-edged passage in which James makes readiness to act only the test of belief and then, in the same breath, makes it what faith *is*. What these passages show is that *James* thought that "believe" was the right word, and that is hardly in question. They do little, however, to show that Miller is correct in thinking that it *is* the right word.

James's response to Miller's paper was much less helpful than it might have been. "Foolish review of it by Miller in Int. J. of Ethics,"[18] he wrote. His suggestion was that Miller had been misled by the word "Will" in his title. "Had I, instead of that inglorious title, called it 'a critique of pure faith' or something like that, those criticisms would have no ground to stand on."[19] Perhaps "will" was a bad choice, and perhaps some criticisms depended on it, although Miller did not think so. It was certainly an odd word if one meant only "all such factors of belief as fear and hope, prejudice and passion, imitation and partisanship, the circumpressure of our caste and set."[20] Miller was surely right, however, in holding that James's doctrine is, at the very least, about letting these various things be factors in what he called "belief," and that this letting is a volitional decision.[21] In any event, avoiding the word "will" and substituting "faith" for "belief" would have done nothing at all to dispel Miller's difficulty over whether the doctrine was a will to believe or a will to make believe one.

In Miller's second paper, the verdict on James's doctrine has not changed. Willing to believe is condemned as "the will to deceive oneself,"[22] the adoption of "a procedure of hypnotizing one's self into a belief."[23] The understanding of the doctrine has not changed either. It is about willing to believe, not something other than belief, and it is as that that Miller condemns it. Some doubt about the interpretation persists, however, surfacing clearly in his discussion of James's "confusion between faith and hypothesis."[24] These are not, he rightly says, one and the same thing. He goes further. They are mutually exclusive, although, he adds, a person may entertain a proposition "at once as a partial belief and as a hypothesis ... Prompted by his partial unbelief he recognizes that the idea must be put to trial; prompted by his partial belief he has chosen it as the one to try."[25] The doubt about the interpretation then manifests itself in the following remark: "But the confusion of these two leads to James's never quite clearing up the question, 'What would be your believer's real state of mind; how far would it be merely a course of action, devout attitude, etc.? How far is it comparable in degree of assurance to the prayer, O God, if there is a God, save my soul if I have a soul?'"[26]

What if James, in response to Miller's first paper, had cleared up that question, saying that by "faith" or "belief" he had meant no more than "working hypothesis"? Subject to two provisos, Miller would have found the thrust of the essay unobjectionable. James would be contending that we are free to take any doctrine as an hypothesis and live accordingly, fully recognizing that it is only an hypothesis, and watching to see if life supplies any confirmation of it. To that claim, he would have agreed, there could be no objection unless on the ground of some want of sufficient initial probability in the particular doctrine to justify conforming one's life to it, or on the ground that life could not supply confirmation.[27] He would still have insisted, however, that by "faith" or "belief" religious people do not mean "working hypothesis," and that an apology for the conscientious agnostic, for the religious inquirer, falls short of being an apology for faith.

What if James's reply had been the different one that he had meant only that it is foolish not to bet on God's existence? Miller would have allowed the general claim that when decision has to be pure gamble and an immediate benefit attaches to betting one way, it is foolish not to bet that way. He would not have allowed, however, that the religious option is a case in point. He rejected the claim that theism is "a subject in which one has no evidence and can get none."[28] He would also have deplored calling "belief" something that is not belief – be it hypothesizing or betting – and he would have insisted that an apology for betting on God's existence does not amount to an apology for faith.

James, of course, did not clear the question up, or even try. He blamed "will" for his troubles, suggested we read "right" in place of it, and left the question about "believe" severely alone. The result is that Miller and

Ducasse, in company with most critics, take the essay to be about a right and about belief. In response, Miller is adamant that there is no right to believe, or try to believe, what the evidence does not favour, but his attitude softens if "believe" is replaced by any of "take as an hypothesis," "act as if true," or "bet on." All of these, he is satisfied, are different from belief, and, were James's essay about any one of them, there would be "no departure from ordinary logical principles as to belief."[29] So far, he is undoubtedly right: acting on a proposition, taking it as an hypothesis, betting on it are, all of them, different from believing it. Miller is also satisfied that faith is or involves believing that God exists and that a case made, therefore, for any of those other things, for anything other than believing, is not a case for faith. He is less clearly right about that. Ducasse comes close to calling that position in question, but he does not do more than come close. Despite picking out as its "one sound point" its recognition that decisions sometimes have to be pure gamble, he is not content to read James's apology for faith as an apology for gambling on God's existence. For him, too, to be an apology for faith, it has to be an apology for believing.

Neither Miller nor Ducasse, in sum, challenge the assumption that faith is belief. What they do is make clear that James's essay will read better if that assumption is rejected. By doing so, they compel the question whether it can be rejected, and that is what makes them especially valuable as critics.

Conclusion

Conclusion

Our study has revolved around two questions. One is whether James's will-to-believe doctrine is a *right*-to-believe doctrine. The other is whether it is a right-to-*believe* doctrine. Orthodoxy, with support from James himself, says yes to both questions. It is clearly mistaken on the first one. What James affirmed is an obligation, not just a right, and that obligation is a prudential, not a moral one. The doctrine begins, I have argued, and continues as a foolish-not-to-believe one. In response to Huxley and Clifford, it does quickly become a foolish-not-to-believe-*and*-not-immoral-to-believe doctrine. The addition is certainly important; but it is not all-important, for the moral claim is far from being a replacement for the original prudential one. That is what fails to be captured in the right-to-believe title.

The other question, whether the doctrine is really about belief, is a more difficult one. It arose some time ago, but we set it aside temporarily to go beating about in some neighbouring fields;[1] and what has flown out from them has served only to confirm the central importance of the question. So we return to it now. Two things make it difficult. One is that the doctrine itself changes. In the early papers the claim is, unquestionably, about belief. It would be foolish of A.C. not to attempt the leap. It would be foolish of him not to believe, for, by believing he improves his chances of success. When the appeal to self-verifying beliefs ceases to have a place, however, as it does when the option is the religious one, the term "belief" persists although there is no longer any place for it either.

The other source of difficulty is the variety of ways in which James describes his topic. His topic is belief, but because it is religious belief, it is faith, and because it is religious belief or faith, it is sometimes believing theism, sometimes betting on it, and sometimes taking it as a working hypothesis. Unhelpfully, James did not choose between these different things: he chose all of them. We now know what made him careless of the differences between them, but the differences are real and important. If p turns out to be false and I believed it, I am surprised but not necessarily disappointed. If I gambled on it, I am disappointed but not necessarily surprised. If I had taken it as an hypothesis, I am not necessarily surprised nor necessarily disappointed either. My purpose was to find out whether p, and I am satisfied to have an answer, no matter what it is. How, then, is one to deal with the question what James's doctrine is about? The only safe answer is to reply that it is about all of the things that have been listed. It is not a helpful answer, however, for what we want to know is which one of them it is about and how to go about deciding that. The way to decide it, I suggest, is to consider which conclusion the argument, James's argument, supports best. That done, we have only one of several possible interpretations of his text, but the most charitable one and also the most defensible one.

It is as an argument for belief that James's case has been widely understood and widely criticized. Russell made the main point as well as anyone. At a fork in the road, I must take one way or the other to have any chance of reaching my destination. I cannot afford just to sit there: I am faced with a forced option. Suppose no signs are posted. In that case, I act on one or other of the two possible hypotheses, but I do not believe either that the way I have chosen leads to my destination or that it does not. The option, as Russell put it, is forced "from the point of view of action."[2] It is not forced from the point of view of belief. Although I cannot afford to suspend action, I can well afford to suspend belief. So, if James's argument is to be one for believing theism, he will have to argue that the option posed by theism is forced, and momentous too, from the point of view of belief. He gives no such argument. He claims that we do best to make willing advances towards theism, to meet it half-way. It is a recommendation to take theism as a working hypothesis. The reason is that only if we do so, do we have a chance of getting the evidence which will enable us, sometime, to decide about theism on intellectual grounds. That claim does nothing at all to support the conclusion that we do best to believe theism unless, of course, it is one and the same thing to believe theism and to take it as an hypothesis; and these, manifestly, are not the same thing.

The argument fares hardly better as an argument for taking theism as an hypothesis. An hypothesis is a tool of inquiry. As such, it is useful if it advances the inquiry of which it is a part. In order to do that, it must satisfy two conditions. We must be able to say what else will be true, if theism is true. We must also have some way of telling whether that something else is true or not. Much that James writes implies that theism as an hypothesis fails that second test. We cannot tell, for example, how the world is to end, safely at journey's end, or in shipwreck.[3] But just that, he suggests sometimes, is what we must know to know if theism is true or not. Nor can we tell what will be the experience and collective verdict upon it of all who agree to allow their willing nature into the game.[4] But that, his other suggestion is, is what we have to know to determine if theism is true or not.

If I am right, it is as an argument for gambling on theism that James's argument fares best. So understood, it runs like this. Whether theism is true, or atheism, is something we cannot now decide on intellectual grounds; so the wise thing is to suspend belief, to believe neither. If we can suspend belief, however, we cannot suspend action; we have to decide how to live our lives. We can live as if theism were true, or as if atheism were true, or on neither of these principles. Any choice we make is pure gamble. Nevertheless it is foolish not to gamble on theism. That is because an "immediate reward," as Ducasse put it, attaches to the act itself of betting on that side. That reward James called "the strenuous mood." The capacity for it could be activated, he thought, by postulating theism, not just by believing it;[5] and the strenuous life was the best life whether or not it was also the right life.

It will be objected that that account of James's argument makes it say both more than the original does, and also less. Both claims are true. The original does not say that, because the religious option is now intellectu- ally undecidable, we ought to suspend judgment about it; and there is much that it does say that is relevant only to a different argument, one for taking theism as an hypothesis. If the match is imperfect, however, between James's text and the account of it given here, the reason has already been made clear. It is that the original fails to distinguish things which are clearly different and, impossibly, offers itself simultaneously as an argument for believing theism, for taking it as an hypothesis, and for gambling on it. In short, the facts objected are admitted, but the fault is traced to the original, where it belongs.

If I am right about that, then, James's doctrine is neither a duty-to- believe one, nor a right-to-believe one, nor a foolish-not-to-believe one. It is a foolish-not-to-gamble one. If that gives an answer to the exegetical question, however, it simply raises another, no less important one, the question whether an argument for gambling on God is "a justification of faith." It is too large a question to be explored fully here. It is also too important to be passed over in silence. So the remarks that follow sketch only an approach to an answer.

1 Gambling is different from guessing.[6] I can guess at the number that will win the raffle, but I do not gamble unless I buy a ticket. I gamble only if there is something that I put at risk, something that I stand to lose if I am wrong. Gambling, in short, is necessarily connected with acting, with doing something. Guessing is not; nor is believing. It is said that faith

without works is dead, is not faith.[7] If that is right, if faith is necessarily connected with action, that will be some reason for thinking that faith is gamble rather than belief.

2 Gambling excludes knowing. If I know the race is fixed, I do not gamble on Aristotle even if I put my money on him. If I do not know the race is fixed and put my money on him, I gamble even if the race is fixed. That is why I can gamble on something that is already decided. What is necessary is that I should not know how the matter turned out. Some define faith as knowledge of God. If it is that, it follows at once that it is not gamble. More commonly, it is defined as belief, not knowledge. That is how James's schoolboy defined it; and most will agree that he had got something wrong. But what he had got wrong, they will also say, was not the "believing" but only the place of the "not." The smiles of amusement would be smiles of approval on most faces if the order were changed to "believing what you *don't know* is true."

3 Gambling does not exclude believing. Having studied his track record, I may believe that Aristotle will win, and back him to win. I may also back him to win without believing that he will. In that way, gambling is like hoping. Just as I can both hope and believe that p, I can both gamble and believe that p. As I can hope that p without believing it, I can also gamble that p without believing it. If faith is gamble, then, the religious person is not as such a believer, but he may be also a believer. Even if he is not a believer, he will be widely *called* a believer, for most are persuaded that "actions speak louder than words," so that if someone acts on a proposition – as the gambler does – ipso facto he believes it.

4 We call some things "a big gamble," others "not much of a gamble." The distinction turns on two things. If I gamble that p, the gamble is bigger or smaller depending on the probability that p. If it is very probable that p, that makes it less of a gamble than it would otherwise be. If it is very improbable that p, that makes it more of a gamble than it would otherwise be. The size of the gamble depends also on the size of the stake, on the value of what I stand to lose if I am wrong. If it is only a trifle, it is not a big gamble even if the probability that p is very low. If I am putting my life at risk, it is a big gamble, even if the chances are good that I shall come out of it without a scratch. Faith, if it is gamble at all, is a big gamble. That is not because the probability is low that God exists. The problem, there, is to establish what the probability is. Some estimate it so low as to be negligible. Others estimate it so high that they speak of faith as knowledge and certainty; and neither side is much moved by the considerations brought forward by the other. What makes faith a big gamble is the size of the stake. "Go sell your possessions and give to the poor."[8] That was the price to the rich man of the ticket of admission to the game. Staking everything they possess; that was Pascal's description

of the mature in faith. No doubt one can quibble over whether it is "gambling with one's life"; but there is no question that, as described, it is definitely a high-stakes game.

5 Whether something is called a gamble or not a gamble, a big gamble or not much of a gamble depends on the *speaker's* estimate of the stake and of the probabilities. So an agent and an observer may well differ on the size of a gamble, and even on whether it is a gamble at all.[9] Typically, that happens over faith. For the unbeliever, it is too much of a gamble: that game, he says, is not worth the candle. For the believer, it is no gamble at all. He calls it a "sure thing." It does not follow that he is right about that. So called "sure things" can be anything but sure. He may also come to call it no gamble at all because he no longer values the stake the way he did. From saying, "If I lose, I lose all," he now says, "If I lose, I lose nothing."

"Damned if I call that faith."[10] Perhaps that is the right response if James's case is for gambling on God, not for believing. It isn't obvious, however, so it needs argument; and such argument as I have found is impressive only in its weakness. Faith cannot be gamble, it runs, because it is knowledge.[11] Or, faith cannot be gamble because it is belief. Or, faith cannot be gamble because faith is serious.[12] The first two of these simply beg the question. They "prove" that faith is not gamble by assuming that it is something else. The assumption is less plausible in the first case, more plausible in the second. The third assumes that gambling is a frivolity, a pastime only. Sometimes it is, sometimes not. It depends on what one is gambling with. And if faith is gambling with one's life, there is nothing frivolous about it at all. Superficially at least, the case looks better on the other side. Abraham is known as the father of faith. That is because, as Hebrews puts it, "he went out not knowing whither he went."[13] For all the world, it looks like gambling.

Notes

INTRODUCTION

1 James, *The Will to Believe*, Introduction, xv–xxiv. Madden's claim is mistaken. It depends on a failure to recognize that James is sometimes talking prudence and sometimes ethics. The complaint that "James had the unfortunate habit of alternating between his weaker and stronger versions in a confusing way in response to criticisms" (xxiii) and that he "was one of those people who try to please everybody and thereby please nobody" (xxiv) is an unprovoked piece of character assassination. There is nothing either evasive or vacillating in claiming, as James did, that it is foolish not to believe, but not immoral.

2 Price, "Belief and Will," 26. Italics mine. For related discussions, see Ammerman, "Ethics and Belief"; Grant, *Belief and Action*; Price, "Professor Grant on Belief and Action." For history, see Price, *Belief*, 130–156, 238; Livingston, *The Ethics of Belief*.

3 Perry, *Thought and Character* 1:531. The phrase is C. Wright's.

4 James, letter to Peirce, 3 February 1899, quoted in Dooley, "The Nature of Belief," 141–2.

5 Perry, *Thought and Character* 2:236. The critic is John J. Chapman.

6 Ibid., 237.

7 Ibid., 243. The critic is Dickinson S. Miller.

8 Ibid.

9 Ibid., 245. The critic is L.T. Hobhouse.

10 Ibid., 246, 488. The critic is A.E. Taylor.

11 Ibid., 246.

12 Ibid., 504.

13 James, *The Will to Believe*, 13.

14 Singer, "The Pragmatic Use of Language," 31.

15 Earle, "James, William," 245.

16 Ibid. The passage is quoted with approval by Levinson, *Science, Metaphysics and the Chance of Salvation*, 227.
17 James, *Essays in Philosophy*, 29; *The Will to Believe*, 79.
18 Miller, "James's Doctrine of 'The Right to Believe'," 541.
19 Perry, *Thought and Character* 2:244.
20 Ibid., 245, 488.
21 James, *The Will to Believe*, 33.
22 Kauber and Hare, "The Right and Duty to Will to Believe," 329. For a criticism, see Wernham, "Did James have an Ethics of Belief?" See also Nakhnikian, *Introduction to Philosophy*, 283.
23 James, *The Will to Believe*, 30.
24 Muyskens, "James' Defense of a Believing Attitude," 51.
25 Ibid.; Muyskens, *The Sufficiency of Hope*, 100.
26 Perry, *Thought and Character* 2:248.
27 Ibid., 245.
28 Hick, *Philosophy of Religion*, 66; *Faith and Knowledge*, 44, where "unrestricted license" becomes "impressive recommendation."
29 Kauber and Hare, "The Right and Duty to Will to Believe," 334, 336; Singer, "The Pragmatic Use of Language," 31. Singer is as confident that James's thesis is "quite definitely intended to apply" only to self-verifying beliefs as Kauber and Hare are that "the plain fact is he did not restrict his right to believe" to genuine options or self-verifying beliefs.
30 Richard Taylor described James's essay as "perhaps the most widely read essay on the rationality of faith ever written in English." Mill, *Theism*, Introduction, xv.

CHAPTER ONE

1 Perry, *Thought and Character* 1:529.
2 Ibid., 530.
3 Ibid.
4 Ibid.
5 Ibid.
6 Ibid., 531. Italics mine.
7 Madden, *Chauncey Wright*, 43–4.
8 Perry, *Thought and Character* 1:530–1.
9 James, *The Will to Believe*, xvii. Italics mine in "review of Tait." Wright's letter makes no mention of the seating arrangements.
10 Perry, *Thought and Character* 1:530.
11 Ibid., 531. The compliment is paid in the Wundt book-notice. See ibid., 528–32.
12 Ibid., 531.

13 Madden, *Chauncey Wright*, 44–5. The quotation from Wright starts too late. See Perry, *Thought and Character* 1:528–32.

14 Madden, *Chauncey Wright*, 43.

15 Perry, *Thought and Character* 1:529.

16 Ibid., 531.

17 Ibid.

18 Madden, *Chauncey Wright*, 43.

19 James, *The Will to Believe*, xvii.

20 Perry, *Thought and Character* 1:531, 532.

21 Ibid., 531–2.

22 Madden, *Chauncey Wright*, 43.

CHAPTER TWO

1 Renouvier. For his comment, see James, *Essays in Philosophy*, 30–1. The anonymous English translation of James's French, published as Appendix 1, is an infantile effort. The quality of the translation is indicated by the rendering of "vos cahiers hebdomadaires" ("your weekly") by "your hebdomadal pages." Where no translating is involved, it manages to get things wrong. It calls the journal, "*Revue Philosophique*" instead of "*Critique Philosophique*."

2 James, *Collected Essays and Reviews*, 25.

3 Ibid., 23.

4 Clifford, *Lectures and Essays* 2:186.

5 James, *Essays in Philosophy*, 25.

6 Ibid., 200. See James, *The Will to Believe*, 17, for his comment on "pretend."

7 James does "open the door to what can be called wishful thinking," and it is mistaken loyalty to seek to defend him against that "criticism." Davis, "Wishful Thinking and 'The Will to Believe'," 231. The only question is how far he opens it. What is objectionable in Hick's phrase is "unrestricted," and what is important is to say *where* James places the barriers, both in his paper on the subjective method and in his will-to-believe essay. Levinson agrees with Davis, rejecting as "fundamental misunderstanding" criticisms which construe the essay as "supportive of wishful thinking." Levinson, *Science, Metaphysics, and the Chance of Salvation*, 227. To make the position plausible he has – implausibly – to restrict wishful thinking to believing what you know is not true. For another response to Hick, see MacLeod, "James's 'Will to Believe': Revisited."

8 James, *Essays in Philosophy*, 23.

9 Ibid., 24.

10 James, *The Will to Believe*, 80.

11 James, *Essays in Philosophy*, 24; *The Will to Believe*, 80, 53.

12 James, *The Will to Believe*, 80.

13 Ibid., 81.

14 James, *Essays in Philosophy*, 24.

15 Ibid.

16 Ibid., 27.

17 James, *The Will to Believe*, 80.

18 Ibid.; *Essays in Philosophy*, 24; *The Will to Believe*, 29.

19 James, *Essays in Philosophy*, 24; *The Will to Believe*, 80, 53.

20 James, *Essays in Philosophy*, 25.

21 Ibid., 24.

22 James, *The Will to Believe*, 80, 53. Compare Price's remarks that the class is "quite a narrow one," "quite a small class." Price, *Belief*, 355, 361. On the whole topic, see Price, *Belief*, 349–75; Grant, *Belief and Action*; and Price, "Professor Grant on Belief and Action."

CHAPTER THREE

1 James, *The Will to Believe*, 57–89, 34–56.

2 James, *Essays in Philosophy*, 26, note.

3 Ibid., 25.

4 James, *Collected Essays and Reviews*, 12–19. Also worth noting is his comment on Wright's disinterest in such topics, 23.

5 James, *Collected Essays and Reviews*, 18.

6 Ibid., 18–19.

7 James, *Essays in Philosophy*, 26.

8 Ibid.

9 Ibid.

10 Ibid.

11 James, *The Will to Believe*, 54.

12 Ibid.

13 Ibid.

14 Ibid., 55.

15 Ibid., 87.

16 James, *Essays in Philosophy*, 29.

17 Ibid.

18 James, *The Will to Believe*, 84–6.

19 James, *Essays in Philosophy*, 30.

20 Singer claims that "James draws *a sharp distinction*" between self-verifying beliefs and beliefs which are not self-verifying. Singer, "The Pragmatic Use of Language," 31. Italics mine. He holds that James's thesis applies only to the former and recognizes that the belief that God exists is not self-verifying. That is what makes him underplay the religious bearing of James's essay. Kaufmann charges that James "*blurs the distinction*" between self-

verifying and other beliefs, and objects against James that the belief that God exists is not self-verifying. Kaufmann, *Critique of Religion and Philosophy*, 86. Italics mine.

CHAPTER FOUR

1 Miller, "James's Doctrine of 'The Right to Believe'," 552.
2 Nakhnikian, *An Introduction to Philosophy*, 286.
3 Kaufmann, *Critique of Religion and Philosophy*, 86.
4 Perry, *Thought and Character* 2:245, 243; Miller, "James's Doctrine of 'The Right to Believe'," 542, 555.
5 James, *The Will to Believe*, 13.
6 Ibid., 20.
7 Ibid., 24.
8 Ibid., 25.
9 Ibid., 29.
10 Ibid.
11 Ibid. See note 20 to chapter 3.
12 Ibid., 20.
13 Ibid., 15.
14 I know of no commentator who has drawn attention to this disparity between James's definition of "forced" and his use of the term. For a suggestive treatment of "cannot," see Price, "Belief and Will," 7; "Now 'cannot' *is* sometimes an abbreviation for 'cannot afford to'."

CHAPTER FIVE

1 James, *The Will to Believe*, 14.
2 Ibid.
3 Ibid., 14–15.
4 Ibid., 15. Levinson transfers "momentous" from options to decisions, and interprets it much too loosely: "Decisions are 'momentous' insofar as they generate some sort of experienceable difference." Levinson, *Science, Metaphysics and the Chance of Salvation*, 222; *The Religious Investigations of William James*, 52.
5 James, *The Will to Believe*, 30. Ayer's comment that James's argument "works both ways," that it "gives exactly the same licence to the atheist as to the theist," overlooks the role of "momentous." Ayer, *The Origins of Pragmatism*, 193.
6 James, *The Will to Believe*, 30.
7 Nakhnikian adopts this line. "But why does James include the word 'yet'? Does he mean to imply that some day science may be able to confirm or disconfirm that affirmation? It seems obvious that science can never either

confirm or disconfirm that statement, and I shall continue the discussion on that assumption." Nakhnikian, *An Introduction to Philosophy*, 280. Kaufmann agrees. "And what are we to make of his concession that this affirmation 'cannot *yet* be verified scientifically'? He writes as if 'the religious hypothesis' were a more or less scientific hypothesis for which no crucial experiment had been devised as yet: one almost gets the feeling that a colleague is working on it even now in the next room, that verification is around the corner, and that we should be stupid if we did not take a chance on it without delay." Kaufmann, *Critique of Religion and Philosophy*, 85. With Kaufmann's "is around the corner," contrast James's frequently repeated warning that hypotheses like the religious one "pourront rester sujettes au doute pendant bien des siècles encore." James, *Essays in Philosophy*, 29. With his conjecture about the *venue* of the experiment, contrast James's placing of it in the market-place. James, *The Will to Believe*, 8.

8 James, *The Will to Believe*, 102, 8.
9 Ibid., 8.
10 James, *The Principles of Psychology* 2:1215–80.
11 Ibid., 1233–4.
12 Ibid., 1237, 1262.
13 Ibid., 1262.
14 Ibid., 1229, 1233.
15 Ibid., 1237.
16 Ibid., 1230–6.
17 Ibid., 1262.
18 For a somewhat fuller discussion, see Wernham, "Ayer's James," 299–302.
19 James *The Principles of Psychology* 2:1239.
20 Ibid., 1262.

CHAPTER SIX

1 James, *The Will to Believe*, 29–30.
2 Kaufmann comments: "Surely, no religion really says what James here claims 'religion says.' But if it did, what exactly would it be saying? What does it mean to say that 'the best things are the more eternal things'? 'Best' is vague, and 'more eternal' comes close to being nonsense: either something is eternal or it is not. To add that the best things are 'the overlapping things' and 'throw the last stone so to speak' only adds further mystification. Is James referring to God but embarrassed to say so?" Kaufmann, *Critique of Religion and Philosophy*, 84. See note 7 to my chapter 5 for comment on the rest of the passage.
3 Findlay, "Can God's Existence be Disproved?" 179–81.
4 James, *The Will to Believe*, 29.
5 Ibid., 31.

6 Ibid., 30.
7 Ibid., 33.
8 Ibid., 31.
9 Ibid., 33.
10 Ibid.
11 Ibid., 30.
12 Ibid., 31.
13 Ibid.
14 Ibid.
15 Ibid.
16 Nakhnikian, *An Introduction to Philosophy*, 280; Kaufmann, *Critique of Religion and Philosophy*, 85. See note 7 to my chapter 5.
17 Santayana, *Character and Opinion in the United States*, 87.
18 Singer's case would have been better, but still imperfect, if he had sought to connect with his pragmatic use of language, not "The Will to Believe," but James's paper on the subjective method.
19 Perry is entirely in the spirit of William James when he defends "non-evidential belief" on the ground, among others, that "faith is sometimes a means of obtaining evidence," and when he adds that: "To find evidence it is necessary to believe in advance that the evidence is there … " *In the Spirit of William James*, 190–1. See also MacLeod, "James's 'Will to Believe': Revisited," 163; and Beard, " 'The Will to Believe' Revisited," 172.

CHAPTER SEVEN

1 Day, "Hope," 99–100, paraphrased. See also Price, "Some Considerations about Belief," 236, 243; and Woozley, *Theory of Knowledge*, 185.
2 Price, "Some Considerations about Belief," 237–8; *Belief*, 208–212.
3 Braithwaite is a good example. "Like moral belief, it [religious belief] is not a species of ordinary belief, of belief in a proposition." Braithwaite, *An Empiricist's View of the Nature of Religious Belief*, 32.
4 Flew, Hare and Mitchell, "Theology and Falsification."
5 See my chapter 13.
6 James, *The Will to Believe*, 32.
7 Ibid.
8 Ibid.
9 Ibid., 16.
10 Ibid., 30.
11 Ibid., 31.
12 Ibid.
13 Perry, *Thought and Character* 2:243.
14 Ibid., 244.
15 James, *The Will to Believe*, 13. Italics mine.

16 Ibid. Italics mine.

17 Ibid., 32, note. Italics mine.

18 Ibid. Italics mine.

CHAPTER EIGHT

1 James. *The Will to Believe*, 76.

2 James, *Essays in Philosophy*, 30.

3 By "not likely" I mean "not *more* probable than not."

4 James, *The Will to Believe*, 79.

5 James, *Essays in Philosophy*, 29.

6 James, *The Will to Believe*, 79.

7 James, *Essays in Philosophy*, 29.

8 James, *The Will to Believe*, 79.

9 Ibid. See note 18 of my chapter 10 for discussion of the rest of James's sentence.

10 Ibid.

11 James, *The Principles of Psychology* 2:913.

12 Ibid., 914, 917.

13 Ibid., 949, note; "The Psychology of Belief," 352.

14 James, *The Will to Believe*, 14.

15 Ibid., 15.

16 Ibid., 32, note.

17 The phrase is borrowed from Hume's *Treatise*, bk. 1, part 3, sec. 2, 81.

CHAPTER NINE

1 Singer, "The Pragmatic Use of Language," 32, note.

2 Clifford, *Lectures and Essays* 2:186. The analysis given is of Clifford's first section, called "The Duty of Inquiry."

3 Clifford, *Lectures and Essays* 2:178.

4 Ibid., 189.

5 James, *Collected Essays and Reviews*, 11. Harvey repeats James's error. "Now if all believing either has to be fully justified (screwed up to the standards authorizing 'I know'), or is immoral, *as Clifford's view dictates ...*" Harvey, "The Ethics of Belief Reconsidered," 413–4. Italics mine.

6 James, *The Will to Believe*, 102.

7 Ibid., 80.

8 Clifford, *Lectures and Essays* 2:189.

9 James, *The Will to Believe*, 88.

10 Ibid.

11 Ibid., 78–9.

12 Ibid., 78.

13 Ibid., 32, note.

CHAPTER TEN

1 For a more technical exposition, see the valuable article, Hacking, "The Logic of Pascal's Wager."
2 James, *The Will to Believe*, 16.
3 Pascal, *Pascal's Pensées*, 119.
4 Ibid.
5 Ibid.
6 Ibid., 121.
7 Ibid.
8 Ibid.
9 Cargile, "Pascal's Wager," 250–2.
10 James, *The Will to Believe*, 16.
11 Ibid., 16–17.
12 Ibid., 30.
13 Ibid., 13.
14 Mrs Fairchild advised investing in the bank of the Lord because it paid the highest dividends. See A.D. Lindsay, *The Moral Teaching of Jesus*, 57, 51; also, C.C.J. Webb, *Pascal's Philosophy of Religion*, 56–7.
15 James, *The Will to Believe*, 30.
16 Pascal, *Pascal's Pensées*, 121, 123. Italic mine.
17 James, *The Will to Believe*, 30. Italics mine.
18 Ibid., 79–80.
19 Pascal, *Pascal's Pensées*, 117.
20 Ibid., 119.
21 In holding that Pascal has not been used as a foil for James, I do not deny, of course, that some critics have noted resemblances. Leslie Stephen and Santayana, to mention only two early ones, saw James's essay as duplicating errors made by Pascal.

CHAPTER ELEVEN

1 Bain, *Mental and Moral Science*, 3rd ed., Appendix, Note on Belief, 100.
2 Braithwaite, "The Nature of Believing," 133, note 2. Cross agrees. See his "Alexander Bain," 8, 12. For other views, see Bradley, *Logic* 1:20, note; and Fisch, "Alexander Bain and the Genealogy of Pragmatism," 422.
3 Bain, *Mental and Moral Science*, 372. See also *Chambers Encyclopaedia* 1:7–9.
4 Bain, *Mental and Moral Science*, 372.
5 Cross, "Alexander Bain," 8–10.
6 Bain, *Mental and Moral Science*, 372.
7 Ibid., 373.
8 Ibid.
9 Ibid., 374.

10 Ibid.

11 Ibid.

12 Ibid., 372.

13 Bain, *The Emotions and the Will*, 3rd ed., 511–18. Page 513 is headed, "Primitive Credulity and Acquired Scepticism." Page 583 of the 1st ed. is captioned, "We believe first and prove afterwards." See also Price, *Belief*, 212–4.

14 Bain, *The Emotions and the Will*, 1st ed., 584.

15 Ibid., 583.

16 Braithwaite, "The Nature of Believing," 133, note 2; "a tendency to action is no longer asserted to be the *differentia* of belief."

17 Bain, *The Emotions and the Will*, 3rd ed., 507.

18 Bain, "Critical Notice of Sully, *Sensation and Intuition*," 147.

19 Mill, James, *Analysis of the Phenomena of the Human Mind* 1:394. Bain's note on Belief is note 107, 393–402.

20 Bain, *Mental and Moral Science*, Appendix, 100.

21 Ibid., 371.

22 Ibid., 374. See also Mill, *Analysis* 1:394.

23 Bain, *The Emotions and the Will*, 3rd ed., 536.

24 Ibid. Italics mine.

25 James, *The Principles of Psychology* 2:917. James's distinction between the "way of analysis" and the "way of history" corresponds to Sully's one between "analysing a mental state into other and simpler states, and assigning to it certain pre-existent states as its conditions." Sully, "The Development of Belief," 126.

26 James, *The Principles of Psychology* 2:946–7.

27 Harvey makes this the major point in his criticism of Clifford. He cites Wittgenstein and Polanyi, but not Bain, in favour of the view that, "We begin by believing and we must have grounds for doubting." He claims that collapse of "the assumption that it is possible to justify all of our beliefs" illustrates the great conceptual gulf between the Victorian intellectual and his modern counterpart. Harvey, "The Ethics of Belief Reconsidered," 410, 408. If so, Bain was much ahead of his time, for, chronologically (1818–1903) he is a Victorian if any one is. His primitive credulity doctrine, incidentally, predates Clifford's essay.

CHAPTER TWELVE

1 Perry, *Thought and Character* 2:209. The date of the letter is 30 November 1897.

2 James, *The Letters of William James* 2:44.

3 The phrase is Schiller's: see his "William James," 41. For a different explanation, see Passmore, *A Hundred Years of Philosophy*, 101.

4 Gallie, *Peirce and Pragmatism*, 26.

5 Taylor, "Some Side Lights on Pragmatism," 44–6.

6 Perry, *Thought and Character* 2:488.

7 Taylor, "Some Side Lights on Pragmatism," 47.

8 Perry, *Thought and Character* 2:248–9. The request was made by H.M. Kallen.

9 Gallie, *Peirce and Pragmatism*, 26.

10 Ibid., 27.

11 In his letter to Peirce, 3 February 1899, James wrote of it as "a lecture of mine in California wherein I flourished the flag of your principle of Pragmatism." See, also, James, *Pragmatism*, 28–9.

12 James, *Pragmatism*, 143.

13 Ibid.

14 Ibid.

15 Russell, *Philosophical Essays*, 120.

16 Ibid., 95.

17 Aiken, "William James," 243–4.

18 James, *The Meaning of Truth*, 146.

19 Ibid., 147.

20 James, *Collected Essays and Reviews*, 434.

21 Russell, *Philosophical Essays*, 120.

22 Notice, however, his concession that Peirce's English ancestors "have many of them no doubt been too sweeping in their negations." James, *Collected Essays and Reviews*, 435.

23 James, *The Letters of William James* 2:295.

24 James, *Pragmatism*, 104.

25 Perry, *Thought and Character* 2:475. For different accounts, see Miller, "James's Doctrine of 'The Right to Believe'," 545; Ayer, *The Origins of Pragmatism*, 196–207; White, *Science and Sentiment in America*, 202–16. On Ayer, see Wernham, "Ayer's James."

26 Perry, *Thought and Character* 2:468.

27 Ibid., 249.

28 Ibid.

29 Ibid., 1:654, 322–4.

30 Renouvier, *Traité de Psychologie Rationelle* 2:84.

31 Ibid., 137.

32 Ibid.

33 Ibid.

CHAPTER THIRTEEN

1 James, letter to Peirce, 3 February 1899, quoted in Dooley, "The Nature of Belief," 141–2.

2 Perry, *Thought and Character* 2:245–6.
3 Hare and Madden, "William James, Dickinson Miller and C.J. Ducasse,"
  116. I rely on their paper for the text of the correspondence, but not for
  the interpretation of it. For their interpretation, see their full title and their
  concluding comment, 126–8. A revised version of Miller's second paper
  is included in his book, *Philosophical Analysis and Human Welfare*, 281–
  311.
4 Hare and Madden, "William James, Dickinson Miller and C.J. Ducasse,"
  123.
5 Ibid. Italics mine.
6 Ibid., 118.
7 Ibid., 117.
8 Ibid., 118.
9 Ibid., 117.
10 Ibid.
11 Ibid., 117–18.
12 Ibid., 126; for Ducasse, 125.
13 Miller, " 'The Will to Believe' and the Duty to Doubt," 183.
14 Ibid.
15 Ibid., 184.
16 Ibid.
17 Ibid., 185.
18 James, letter to Peirce, 3 February 1899, quoted in Dooley, "The Nature of
  Belief," 141–2.
19 Ibid. See also Perry, *Thought and Character* 2:243, 244.
20 James, *The Will to Believe*, 18.
21 Miller, "James's Doctrine of 'The Right to Believe'," 556.
22 Ibid., 553.
23 Ibid., 556.
24 Ibid., 547.
25 Ibid.
26 Ibid.
27 Ibid., 547–8.
28 Hare and Madden, "William James, Dickinson Miller and C.J. Ducasse,"
  123.
29 Miller, "James's Doctrine of 'The Right to Believe'," 548.

CONCLUSION

1 Chap. 8, 105.
2 Russell, *Philosophical Essays*, 84.
3 James, *Collected Essays and Reviews*, 420–3.
4 Ibid., 79.

5 James, *The Will to Believe*, 161.

6 Perry, *Thought and Character* 2:242–3.

7 James 2:20 AV.

8 Matt. 19:21 NEB.

9 Hazleton, "Pascal's Wager Argument," 113, 116.

10 See Introduction, note 5.

11 Hick, *Faith and Knowledge*, 42.

12 Ibid., 40. See also O'Connell, *William James on the Courage to Believe*, 25–31, 49.

13 Heb. 11:8 AV.

Bibliography

The bibliography is limited to works which have been cited in the text or in the notes. Its purpose is to identify cited titles more fully than is done in the notes.

Aiken, H.D. "American Pragmatism Reconsidered, 2: William James." *Commentary* 34, no. 3 (1962): 238–46.

Ammerman, R.R. "Ethics and Belief." *Proceedings of the Aristotelian Society* 65 (1964–5): 257–66.

Ayer, A.J. *The Origins of Pragmatism*. London: Macmillan and Co. 1968.

Bain, A. *The Emotions and the Will*. London: John W. Parker and Son 1859.

– *The Emotions and the Will*. 3rd (1875) ed. London: Longmans, Green and Co. 1880.

– *Mental and Moral Science*. 3rd (1872) ed. London: Longmans, Green and Co. 1879.

– "Belief." *Chambers Encyclopaedia*. London: W. and R. Chambers 1861.

– "Critical Notice: *Sensation and Intuition*." *Fortnightly Review* o.s. 22, n.s. 16 (1 July 1874): 146–8.

Beard, R.W. "'The Will to Believe' Revisited." *Ratio* 8, no. 2 (1966): 169–79.

Bradley, F.H. *The Principles of Logic*. 2 vols. 2nd ed. London: Oxford University Press 1920.

Braithwaite, R.B. *An Empiricist's View of the Nature of Religious Belief*. Cambridge: Cambridge University Press 1955.

– "The Nature of Believing." *Proceedings of the Aristotelian Society* 33 (1932–3): 129–46.

Cargile, J. "Pascal's Wager." *Philosophy* 41, no. 157 (1966): 250–7.

Clifford, W.K. *Lectures and Essays*. 2 vols. Edited by Leslie Stephen and Sir Frederick Pollock. London: Macmillan and Co. 1879.

Cross, R.C. "Alexander Bain." *Proceedings of the Aristotelian Society* supp. vol. 44 (1970): 1–13.

Cushman, R.E. and E. Grislis, editors. *The Heritage of Christian Thought*. New York: Harper and Row 1965.

Davis, S.T. "Wishful Thinking and 'The Will to Believe'." *Transactions of the C.S. Peirce Society* 8, no. 4 (1972): 231–45.

Day, J.P. "Hope." *American Philosophical Quarterly* 6, no. 2 (1969): 89–102.

Dooley, P.K. "The Nature of Belief: The Proper Context for James' 'The Will to Believe'." *Transactions of the C.S. Peirce Society* 8, no. 3 (1972): 141–51.

Earle, W.J. "James, William." *The Encyclopedia of Philosophy* 8 vols. New York: Macmillan Publishing Co. and The Free Press 1967.

Findlay, J.N. "Can God's Existence be Disproved?" *Mind* 57, no. 226 (1948): 176–83.

Fisch, Max. "Alexander Bain and the Genealogy of Pragmatism." *Journal of the History of Ideas* 15, no. 3 (1954): 413–44.

Flew, A.G.N., R.M. Hare and B. Mitchell. "Theology and Falsification: a Symposium." *New Essays in Philosophical Theology*. Edited by A. Flew and A. MacIntyre. London: S.C.M. 1955.

Gallie, W.B. *Peirce and Pragmatism*. Harmondsworth: Penguin Books 1952.

Grant, C.K. *Belief and Action*. Durham: University of Durham 1960.

Hacking, Ian. "The Logic of Pascal's Wager." *American Philosophical Quarterly* 9, no. 2 (1972): 186–92.

Hare, P.H. and E.H. Madden. "William James, Dickinson Miller and C.J. Ducasse on the Ethics of Belief." *Transactions of the C.S. Peirce Society* 4, no. 3 (1968): 115–29.

Harvey, V.A. "The Ethics of Belief Reconsidered." *Journal of Religion* 59, no. 4 (1979): 406–20.

Hazleton, R. "Pascal's Wager Argument." *The Heritage of Christian Thought*. Edited by Cushman and Grislis, 108–26.

Hick, J. *Faith and Knowledge*. London: Macmillan 1967.

– *Philosophy of Religion*. Englewood Cliffs: Prentice-Hall 1963.

Hume, D. *A Treatise of Human Nature*. 2 vols. London: Everyman's Library. J.M. Dent and Sons 1911.

James, William. *Collected Essays and Reviews*. Edited by R.B. Perry. New York: Longmans, Green and Co. 1920.

– *Essays in Philosophy*. Cambridge, Mass. and London, England: Harvard University Press 1978.

– *The Letters of William James*. 2 vols. Edited by his son Henry James. Boston: The Atlantic Monthly Press 1920.

– *The Meaning of Truth*. Cambridge, Mass. and London, England: Harvard University Press 1975.

– *Pragmatism*. Cambridge, Mass. and London, England: Harvard University Press 1975.

– *The Principles of Psychology*. 3 vols. Cambridge, Mass. and London, England: Harvard University Press 1981.

– *The Will to Believe and Other Essays in Popular Philosophy.* Cambridge, Mass. and London, England: Harvard University Press 1979.
– "The Psychology of Belief." *Mind* 14, no. 55 (1889): 321–52.
Kauber, P. and P.H. Hare. "The Right and Duty to Will to Believe." *Canadian Journal of Philosophy* 4, no. 2 (1974): 327–43.
Kaufmann, W. *Critique of Religion and Philosophy.* New York: Harper and Brothers 1958.
Levinson, H.S. *The Religious Investigations of William James.* Chapel Hill: University of North Carolina Press 1981.
– *Science, Metaphysics and the Chance of Salvation.* A.A.R. Dissertation Series no. 24. Missoula, Montana: Scholars Press 1978.
Lindsay, A.D. *The Moral Teaching of Jesus.* London: Hodder and Stoughton 1937.
Livingston, J.C. *The Ethics of Belief.* A.A.R. Studies in Religion no. 9. Missoula, Montana: Scholars Press 1974.
MacLeod, W.J. "James's 'Will to Believe': Revisited." *Personalist* 48, no. 2 (1967): 149–66.
Madden, E.H. *Chauncey Wright and the Foundations of Pragmatism.* Seattle: University of Washington Press 1963.
Mill, James. *Analysis of the Phenomena of the Human Mind* with notes illustrative and critical by Alexander Bain, Andrew Findlater and George Grote. 2 vols. Edited with additional notes by John Stuart Mill. London: Longmans, Green, Reader and Dyer 1869.
Mill, J.S. *Theism.* Edited with an introduction by Richard Taylor. Indianapolis: Bobbs-Merrill 1957.
Miller, D.S. *Philosophical Analysis and Human Welfare.* Edited by L.D. Easton. Dordrecht, Holland: D. Reidel Publishing Co. 1975.
– "James's Doctrine of 'The Right to Believe'." *The Philosophical Review* 51, no. 6 (1942): 541–58.
– "'The Will to Believe' and the Duty to Doubt." *International Journal of Ethics* 9 no. 2 (1898–9): 169–95.
Muyskens, J.L. *The Sufficiency of Hope.* Philadelphia: Temple University Press 1979.
– "James' Defense of a Believing Attitude in Religion." *Transactions of the C.S. Peirce Society* 10, no. 1 (1974): 44–53.
Nakhnikian, G. *An Introduction to Philosophy.* New York: Alfred A. Knopf 1967.
O'Connell, R.J. *William James on the Courage to Believe.* New York: Fordham University Press 1984.
Pascal, B. *Pascal's Pensées* with an English translation, brief notes and introduction by H.F. Stewart. London: Routledge and Kegan Paul 1950.
Passmore, J. *A Hundred Years of Philosophy.* Harmondsworth: Penguin Books 1968.
Perry, R.B. *In the Spirit of William James.* Bloomington: Indiana University Press 1958.

- *The Thought and Character of William James.* 2 vols. Boston: Little, Brown and Co. 1935.
Price, H.H. *Belief.* London: Allen and Unwin 1969.
- "Belief and Will." *Proceedings of the Aristotelian Society* supp. vol. 28 (1954): 1–26.
- "Professor Grant on Belief and Action." *The Durham University Journal* 53, no. 3 (1961): 97–102.
- "Some Considerations about Belief." *Proceedings of the Aristotelian Society* 35 (1934–5): 229–52.
Renouvier, Ch. *Essais de Critique Générale: Deuxième Essai: Traité de Psychologie Rationelle d'après les Principes du Criticisme.* 2 vols. Paris: Librairie Armand Colin 1912.
Russell, B. *Philosophical Essays.* Rev. ed. London: Allen and Unwin 1966.
Santayana, G. *Character and Opinion in the United States.* New York: W.W. Norton and Co. 1967.
Schiller, F.C.S. "William James." *Quarterly Review* 236, no. 468 (1921): 24–41.
Singer, M.G. "The Pragmatic Use of Language and The Will to Believe." *American Philosophical Quarterly* 8, no. 1 (1971): 24–34.
Stephen, L. "The Will to Believe." *The Agnostic Annual* (1898): 14–22.
Sully, J. *Sensation and Intuition.* London: Henry S. King and Co. 1874.
- "The Development of Belief." *The Westminster Review* O.S.97 N.S.41 (Jan. 1872): 121–63.
Taylor, A.E. "Some Side Lights on Pragmatism." *McGill University Magazine* 3, no. 2 (1904): 44–66.
Webb, C.C.J. *Pascal's Philosophy of Religion.* Oxford: Clarendon Press 1929.
Wernham, J.C.S. "Alexander Bain on Belief." *Philosophy* 61, no. 236 (1986): 262–6.
- "Ayer's James." *Religious Studies* 12, no. 3 (1976): 291–302.
- "Bain's Recantation." *Journal of the History of Philosophy* 24, no. 1 (1986): 107–11.
- "Did James have an Ethics of Belief?" *Canadian Journal of Philosophy* 6, no. 2 (1976): 287–97.
White, Morton. *Science and Sentiment in America.* London: Oxford University Press 1972.
Woozley, A.D. *Theory of Knowledge.* London: Hutchinson University Library 1973.

Index

I have used the following abbreviations; Q.C. in place of "Quelques Considérations sur la Méthode Subjective," and W.B. in place of "The Will to Believe."

103; and deciding, 57–8; and belief in James, 65, 74, 77, 101; not prohibited by Clifford, 69, 74; and belief in Pascal, 75–7; and belief, 84; and belief in Ducasse, 94–6; and belief in Miller, 97–8; whether faith, 103–5
Gaming table, 58, 80
Genuine option, 7, 34, 35; religious option as, 43, 46. *See also* Forced option; Living option; Momentous option; Option
Guessing, 69, 74, 103

History, 64, 116n25
Hope, 7, 51, 96, 104
Hypothesis: faith as working, 6, 7, 62–4, 79; belief and working, 7, 58, 97, 101; meeting the, half-way, 51–2, 58–9; and the inquirer, 57, 62–4, 84; and deciding, 57–8; taking theism as working, 58–9, 102–3; and belief, 64–5, 69, 97–8; and pragmatism, 89, 90

Idealism. *See* Materialism
Intellectually undecidable option, 4, 7, 34–40 passim, 42–4, 52, 56, 80, 92
Irreversible decision, 41–2

Knowledge, 104, 105

Larceny, 91. *See also* Renouvier
Lectures, Wright's, 11–14, 16
Lessons, 20, 24, 27
Letters: Wright's, 11, 13, 15; James's, 91
Licence, 7. *See also* Wishful thinking
Living option, 7, 41, 43, 80

Materialism, 24, 28–9, 88
Meaning. *See* Definition
Metaphysics, 19, 24, 27, 30, 46, 90
Mill, 86, 89
Miller, 6, 93–8
Misrepresentation, 5, 11, 72–3
Momentous option: meaning of, 4, 7, 40, 42, 111n4; examples of, 41, 42; religion as, 42, 43, 48, 102, 111n5; and Pascal, 80

Nansen, 41–2

Objective method. *See* Subjective method
Obligation: as James's subject, 3, 7, 101; as his subject in 1875, 13, 15–16; as his subject in Q.C., 17–20, 30; as his subject in W.B., 35–6, 38–9, 49, 53, 88, 91; confessed, 87, 92
Optimism, 24–8

Option: definition of, and examples, 40–1; between
propositions or actions, 40–2; decide an, and believe,
48, 50, 52, 54, 55–8, 59. *See also* Genuine option;
Intellectually undecidable option
Orthodoxy, 3, 4, 101, 107n1
Ought. *See* Obligation

Pascal, 4, 75–80, 104; James on, 58, 77–9; as foil for
James, 69, 74, 75, 80
Passional decision, 37–8
Passional nature, 34–5, 40, 43
Passive mind, 73, 74
Peirce, 87, 88, 89
Pessimism. *See* Optimism
Pragmatic use, 6, 113n18
Pragmatism, 4, 87–91
Price, 3
Primitive credulity. *See* Credulity
Prize. *See* Reward
Propositions, James division of, 45–6; religious, 54, 55–6.
See also Option
Prudence, 15, 49, 69, 80
Prudentialism, 80
Prudential obligation. *See* Obligation

Readiness to act: faith as, 60–2, 96. *See also* Action
Recantation, Bain's, 81, 85–6
Religion: and thesis statement, 4, 34; and verifiability,
43–5, 56; as live hypothesis, 79; and pragmatism, 87,
88
Religious belief. *See* Faith
Religious hypothesis: backing the, 7, 58, 78; and
verifiability, 44–6; meeting the, half-way, 59; and
pragmatism, 88
Religious option: and James's thesis, 34; and irre-
versibility, 42; and intellectual undecidability, 42–5,
46, 52, 56, 103; as genuine, 43, 46; as forced and
momentous, 43, 48; and suspending judgment, 51; and
gamble, 95, 97
Renouvier, 4, 17, 23, 25, 87, 91–2
Reward, 75, 76, 94–5, 103
Right: and obligation, 3, 20, 35–6, 38, 48, 49, 53, 74;
as replacement for Will, 6, 33, 54, 97. *See also*
Orthodoxy; Will-to-believe doctrine
Right not to believe, 18, 19
Risk: and suspending judgment, 34, 37–8, 50; belief and,
57, 58; gamble and, 103, 104
Russell, 88, 89, 90, 102

Santayana, 52

Wishful thinking, 7, 18, 20, 24, 73, 109n7
Working hypothesis. *See* Hypothesis
Wright, 11–16
Wundt, 12, 13

Yet, 4, 43–6, 52, 56, 111n7